Language with Altitude

For Andrew & Mark
with grateful thanks
for your exemplary
ministry over many years.

Paul

Language with Altitude

Paddy Gormley

Matador
Unit E2 Airfield Business Park,
Harrison Road, Market Harborough,
Leicestershire. LE16 7UL
Tel: 0116 2792299
Email: books@troubador.co.uk
Web: www.troubador.co.uk/matador
Twitter: @matadorbooks

ISBN 978 1803136 080

British Library Cataloguing in Publication Data.
A catalogue record for this book is available from the British Library.

Printed and bound by CPI Group (UK) Ltd, Croydon, CR0 4YY
Typeset in 14pt Baskerville by Troubador Publishing Ltd, Leicester, UK

Matador is an imprint of Troubador Publishing Ltd

to friends and family
who have stood fast by me

Language with Altitude

Contents

book 1:
finding your feet

book 2:
getting better verse

book 3:
constructive induction

book 4:
stirring words

Evocative language summons memories into the mind's eye. All language is evocative insofar as language is symbolic: we rely on memory to decode the symbols.

Ambiguity enhances the evocative power of language. Metaphors are particularly evocative since they initiate and connect two disparate trains of thought.

The memorability of text increases with its evocative power. Ideas that persist longest in the mind's eye are most likely to become lasting memories.

book 5:
proficiency in poetry

book 6:

persuasive proseverse

book 7:
choosing and using amusing ideas

book 8:
inspiration by limitation

foreword

Inspirational language is an endangered species in this age of instant opinionation and robotic speech. And yet the persuasive power of language is there for the taking by people in all walks of life.

Let us work together, you and I, to preserve and enhance the richness of spoken and written English. Let us speak and write LANGUAGE WITH ALTITUDE.

LANGUAGE WITH ALTITUDE is not just for poets. It's for everyone who needs to exploit the imaginative and persuasive power of English: politicians, poets, presenters, playwrights, performers, persuaders, professors, prose writers, philanderers, philosophers, philanthropists, prelates, priests... people in every walk of life.

LANGUAGE WITH ALTITUDE begins with a primer of verse writing technique, but you'll soon find that it's much more than that.

Whether you're a beginner writer or a practised professional, I hope you will find yourself transported to new heights of creative and analytical writing:

- discover simple, powerful metaphors for the imagination;

- appreciate how your words cause listeners or readers to evoke memories and to construct realistic images in the mind's eye;

- learn to exploit the amazing power of ambiguity in the hidden realm of subtext;

- understand how memory is based on the recognition of patterns from infant days;

- know that patterns of speech-sound touch the emotions by connecting with the primeval in us;

- learn to think clearly with the help of a radical reinterpretation of Aristotle's rules for reasoning;

- put these principles into practice not only in compelling stories, poetry and comic verse, but also inspirational speeches and business reports;

- benefit from countless insights into the principles of thinking, writing and public speaking, with the help of sparkling illustrations of every concept discussed in the text.

I want to make this a personal experience for you. I will speak directly to you and I will lead by example. Most of the text of this volume is written in proseverse: a heightened form of language that reads as fluently and persuasively as any well written prose, but uses hidden rhythms and rhymes: it's LANGUAGE WITH ALTITUDE.

This project began in 1997 as a primer of verse technique for children (now completely rewritten). I had already been developing proseverse in my creative writing for some years.

My first efforts to understand and document the characteristics of metre and rhyme led me to think more deeply about language: how memory is formed, how the creative process works, how the intellectual and emotional spheres interact (or don't), and so on.

I devised a series of metaphors that seemed to explain the workings of memory and the imagination in simple but amazingly powerful terms. These metaphors, in turn, led me to new insights about all sorts of writing, analytical as well as creative.

My ten-year train of thought is reflected in the structure of this volume, as follows.

The first two books, FINDING YOUR FEET and GETTING BETTER VERSE, are concerned with verse technique and basic creative writing skills.

The third and fourth books explore the processes of thought, memory and imagination:

- CONSTRUCTIVE INDUCTION provides a simple model for the creative process based on alternating sessions of inductive and deductive reasoning;

- STIRRING WORDS explains the workings of evocative language and subtext, and considers the characteristics of memorable text.

The following three books consider how these ideas may be applied in a trio of contrasting fields:

- PROFICIENCY IN POETRY is primarily for poets;

- PERSUASIVE PROSEVERSE is intended for writers and public speakers whose aim is to persuade others;

- CHOOSING AND USING AMUSING IDEAS addresses the subject of comedy writing.

In presenting these three diverse disciplines together, my hope is that writers in all fields may appreciate the value of techniques beyond their usual sphere. Professional persuaders, for example, have much to gain by being sometimes poetic and sometimes funny.

The volume ends with INSPIRATION BY LIMITATION, which considers the importance of constraints as a means of firing the imagination.

My aims are twofold:

- I hope to give you a good read, with lots of exciting new discoveries along the way;

- I also mean to inspire you to use these techniques for yourself; I'm hoping that you'll come back to this volume repeatedly, working through the text and the exercises, trying my ideas and using them as a springboard for your own.

introduction
to proseverse

Proseverse sounds like normal speech. It's different, though. In proseverse:

- each sound fits the rhythmic pattern;

- there are hidden rhymes.

We're unaware of all these inner workings when we're listening. That's because the sentences express their meaning clearly: we imagine that we're hearing ordinary prose.

We concentrate on what's being said, not on the technicalities, whereas pure verse—the sort we're used to—has a different emphasis, such that we're more aware of rhythmic patterns.

In a limerick, for instance, we know,
by the pauses that break up the flow,
that there'll be certain times
when we're going to hear rhymes
and we'll know when it's finished—like so.

Proseverse is altogether less predictable and more expressive than pure verse. It is more pleasing to the ear than prose, and easier to commit to memory, with its gentle rhymes and steady rhythms.

Proseverse's greatest strength lies in the fascinating disciplines that it imposes on the writer.

Writing good proseverse is quite a challenge. Every word must be subjected to close scrutiny: of meaning, sound, accentuation, rhythm, context.

The formation of proseverse is like a love affair with English: the discovery of new words, meanings and new sounds enriches understanding of the language.

Proseverse, though, is not exclusively for poets.

There's something in proseverse technique for everyone who needs to speak or write persuasively:

- for those who work with rhythmic speech: composers, actors, singers;

- those who reach out to the public with their speech, who must use pithy, eloquent, amusing, memorable sentences: presenters, business leaders, politicians;

- those who need good English for their first or second language, who must learn correct pronunciation and develop their awareness of the elements of style and usage;

- writers of all sorts who wish to heighten their expressive capabilities or their creative skills;

- or poets who have never fully fathomed the incredible potential of the simple art of writing verse.

So let's get started.

Proseverse sounds like normal speech.
It's different, though. In proseverse:

- each
  sound fits the rhythmic pattern;

- there
  are hidden rhymes.

We're unaware
of all these inner workings when
we're listening. That's because the sentences
express their meaning clearly:
we imagine that we're hearing
ordinary prose.

We concentrate
on what's being said, not on
the technicalities, whereas
pure verse—the sort we're used to—has
a different emphasis, such that
we're more aware of rhythmic patterns.

In a limerick, for instance, we know,
by the pauses that break up the flow,
that there'll be certain times
when we're going to hear rhymes
and we'll know when it's finished—like so.

13

Proseverse is altogether less
predictable and more expressive
than pure verse. It is more pleasing
to the ear than prose, and easier
to commit to memory, with
its gentle rhymes and steady rhythms.

Proseverse's greatest strength lies in
the fascinating disciplines
that it imposes on the writer.
Writing good proseverse is quite
a challenge. Every word must be
subjected to close scrutiny:
of meaning, sound, accentuation,
rhythm, context.

The formation
of proseverse is like a love
affair with English: the discovery
of new words, meanings and
new sounds enriches understanding
of the language.

Proseverse, though,
is not exclusively for poets.
There's something in proseverse technique
for everyone who needs to speak
or write persuasively; for:

14

- those
  who work with rhythmic speech: composers,
  actors, singers;

- those who reach
  out to the public with their speech,
  who must use pithy, eloquent,
  amusing, memorable sentences:
  presenters, business leaders,
  politicians;

- those who need
  good English for their first or second
  language, who must learn correct
  pronunciation and develop
  their awareness of the elements
  of style and usage;

- writers
  of all sorts who wish to heighten
  their expressive capabilities
  or their creative skills;

- and poets who have never fully
  fathomed the incredible
  potential of the simple art
  of writing verse.

So let's get started.

book 1:
finding your feet

book 1:
finding your feet

This book will show you how speech patterns
may be shaped to create natural
and yet distinctly graceful
verse.

You'll learn some simple, basic
rules about the inherent rhythms
of the spoken word.

Then, with
a little practice, you'll find you can easily
write fluent lines of verse like these.

1a. why verse?

Patterns are surprisingly
important. Our humanity
depends on them.

Before we learn
our first words, even, we discern
the pattern of our mother's face
and use this pattern as the basis
for the mental library
of faces that we build as we
grow older.

Before long we teach
ourselves the patterns on which speech
is based. We're able to make sense
of it by building an extensive
catalogue, the more amazing
for our age, of sounds, words, phrases,
tones and grammar.

In the nursery,
the use of rhythmic verse

helps us to underpin this catalogue
with corresponding patterns
of accent and beat.

pattern
recognition

We gain
far more than childish entertainment
from this pattern recognition.

- Verse, based on the repetition
  of a recognisable
  speech rhythm, sounds more musical,
  more pleasing to the ear, than ordinary
  speech.

- Verse is, accordingly,
  more memorable than prose,
  which is why every adult knows
  his or her favourite poetry
  by heart but cannot usually
  recite, with similar exactitude,
  more than a brief extract
  of any favourite novel.

The
enduring popularity
of verse is largely due to our
response to rhyme.

The rhythmic power
of verse increases with the addition
of rhyme words, evenly positioned.

- Listening, we become aware
  of rhyming sounds, and we learn where
  and when the next rhyme's due.

- It's satisfying
  when we get the pattern
  right.

- It's still more so when we
  guess what the next rhyme word will be.

In short, verse is not only fun
but also useful.

Now you understand
these precepts, I hope you'll agree
that verse is not exclusively
for poets. Using verse technique,
you can transform the words you speak
or write on any theme and make
the most mundane text sound like Shakespeare!

1b. rhyme

Verse technique is all
about the rise and fall
of speech. It's sound, not sense
(although true eloquence
depends on both).

Let's start,
then, with the basic particles
of speech-sound: syllables.

The minimal
sound is an open vowel:
that is, sheer, air-powered
sound, unstopped: *a:*, *i:**
and so on.

It is the
addition of the stopped
sounds—consonants—that crops

** a: is the phonetic symbol for a as in arm. i: represents e as in me.
These symbols are used to emphasise the fact that the text refers to
vowel/diphthong sounds rather than alphabetic characters.*

a syllable at either
end or both (or neither).

The *l* and *t* of *lit*
give it a definite
beginning, middle and end
(although sometimes we blend
adjacent syllables:
the end of one may spill
into the next).

To make
a rhyme, we need to take
two syllables based on
the same vowel and end consonants
but different starting
sounds.

Let's take apart
a pair of rhyme words: *sill*
and *shrill*.

* Note how both syllables
  use *i* as in *ill*
  cropped with a tongue-stop *ll*.

  sāmenĕss

* The non-identical
  bits are the *shr* and *s*
  sounds.

24

There's no rhyme unless
the syllables fulfil
both of these principles.

Therefore you can't pair
such words as *fair*, af*fair*
and thorough*fare* together.
It doesn't matter whether
they're spelt differently.
The problem is with the
*f*s sounding all the same.

too much sameness

Nor, strictly speaking, can
a syllable like *plan*
be rhymed with *pram*. The *n*
and *m* sounds aren't identical.
True rhymes depend
on vowel sound and end
stops being in harmony
in every degree.

too much difference

things to do

Analyse rhymes in some of your favourite rhyming
poetry in terms of sameness and difference as
illustrated here. Notice how frequently poets bend or
break these rules!

25

1c. stress patterns

Let's concentrate on rhythm next.

You'll notice, as you read this text,
that half the syllables are stressed
quite firmly and the others less
so.

Note the stress marks:

- ▬ straight marks serve to indicate
  stressed syllables;

- ◗ the ones
  that curve refer to unstressed
  syllables.

The rhythmic quality
comes from the rise and fall
of speech inherent in the alternating
stressed and unstressed sounds.

Stress patterns may, of course, be found
in everyday speech, but these are

26

less rhythmic and less regular.
They lack the sense of evenness
that comes from:

- ● alternating stressed
  and unstressed syllables

- ● or from regular triplets of syllables:
  one stressed per two unstressed.

Verse
technique is all about coercing
rhythms into graceful patterns
based on simple mathematics.

By contrast, the rhythmic patterns of ordinary prose,
though recognisable and attractive to the lover of
language, are more complex and, accordingly, less
engaging than verse patterns.

Prose and verse are both based on stressed and
unstressed syllables. In prose, however, the number of
unstressed syllables per stressed syllable ranges
erratically from nought to four or more.

It's the stressed syllables that give
the text its shape. They are the pivot points.

27

Unstresses are more liquid.
They're passed over lightly, quickly.

Rhyming syllables are always stressed.
The difference that makes the rhyme is pressed
home on the beat, though it is possible
to extend the rhyme with unstressed syllables
that reinforce the sameness.

Take

vanilla

a rhyming pair like *bake* and *shake*.

gorilla

If we add the same unstressed syllable
to each—say, *baking, shaking*—they will still
rhyme, but the sameness goes on longer,
so the rhyme's a little stronger.

The effect is still greater when you
use a stress pattern based upon two
unstressed syllables: *tentacle*,
*pentacle**. Here, the identical

friskier

sounds span three syllables. These

riskier

rhymes are wonderful, but it's not easy
to work with them much of the time.
There aren't many three-syllable rhyme
words in English. I'm proud to have managed to fit
quite a few good ones into the verse opposite.

---

* A pentagram, esp. as a magical symbol (Shorter O.E.D.)

london bridge

From pathways arterial,
early each ferial
day, managerial
types, esoterical
specialists, clerical
staff and professionals
join the processional
matinal ritual,
take their habitual
stroll to their places
of work with briefcases
of matters contractual,
documents factual,
looks on their faces
of mischief, prosperity,
candour, temerity,
some intellectual,
some ineffectual,
minds automatically
wandering erratically:
gardening, annuities,
tort, promiscuity,
broking, astrology,
client psychology.

Arriving thousands sitting at their screens
become the City's wonderful machine.

As for rhymes with four syllables, they're
almost unknown, at least very rare.
One example's *impĕrīoŭsnĕss*
rhyming with *sērīoŭsnĕss*.
This doesn't work if we happen to stress
the fourth syllable, though: say *impĕrīoŭsnēss*.
The *ness*, having acquired a stress of its own, might
be used as a rhymed syllable in its own right.

Many syllables may be expressed
sometimes as stressed and sometimes as unstressed
sounds, according to the context.

Most words (excluding certain monosyllables
like *a* or *an*)
include an accent that is mandatory
in the spoken English language.

Wrongly accented words sound mangled
and unclear (try making *happen* rhyme
with *ten*, *father* with *sir* or *fate* with *climate*).

But some words are not restricted
in this way. The courts cŏnvīct;
the prisoner, though, is a cōnvĭct.

variable
stress

This limited degree
of flexibility
ensures that most words can be made to fit

a regular stress pattern, whether it
is based on one or two unstresses
per stressed syllable. Take *necessary*,
for example. It must start
with a firm accent but, apart
from that, you're free to choose. The *air*
sound may be stressed, viz. *nēcĕssāry̆*,
or it can fit with a pattern of three
syllables, as in *nēcĕssăry̆*.

things to do

Conduct a detailed analysis of the stress patterns of a
few sentences of ordinary prose. Identify alternative
patterns wherever possible.

- Are any of the available alternatives sufficiently
  rhythmical to suggest that the prose could pass for
  verse (whether rhyming or not)?

- Can you improve the rhythm by changing the
  word order and/or substituting different words in
  places?

Conduct a similar analysis of speech patterns in
favourite poems, including poems that look as if they
may not actually be based on verse technique. Are
you always able to find stress patterns that appear to
have been constructed deliberately?

1d. me̅trĕ

A foot, in verse, consists of one
stressed syllable plus any unstressed
syllables immediately before
or after it.

It's best if I ignore
the arcane issue of deciding
where one places the dividing
line between feet.

Think of feet
in terms of one foot for each beat.
That's good enough for this book.

Metre
is the measurement of length of lines.
The number of feet in any line defines
the metre. Verses with two feet
per line, for instance, are in dimeter.
(We'll explore the full list presently.)

In rhyming verse, the line length sets the frequency
of rhyme words. Since each line

must have a rhymed sound as its final
stress, short lines require such densely
packed rhyme words that, though they're immensely
challenging to write,
their sound is most exciting.

Mōno-
mēter's
cōnstant
bēat
means rhȳming
ēvery
tīme
and nēver
pūtting a
fōot wrong.

monometer

Writing
mono-
meter's
quite
a ponderous
feat
and oh
so
slow.

dimeter

Compare dimeter,
(with two feet
per line, like these
lines). It is ea-
sier to write
since it's less tightly
rhymed than mono-
meter. Non-
rhymes make up half
the stresses.

Drafting
takes good crafts-
manship, though the
alacrity
of the resulting
sound is ul-
timately satisfying.

trimeter

Writing rhyming tri-
meter is somewhat less
demanding: just one stress
in three must rhyme. There's more
room to begin exploring
language, introducing
words not just for use
as rhymes, but for their o-
verall sense of appro-
priateness.

The groups of three
stressed syllables are pleasing
to the ear. The triple
rhythm has a skipping,
dancing quality,
and especially when there are three
syllables per foot: that's to say nine
syllables to be heard in each line.

tetrameter

Tetrameter is more sedate.
It has a gently marching gait:
four-square, well balanced, confident
and rhythmically elegant.

Note how musicians often use
this metre ("four-four") in their music.
Line follows line without a pause.
It's pleasing to the ear because
of its primeval mathematics:
powers of two are an emphatic
rhythmic force. We feel the pattern
without conscious thought. Our feet
instinctively tap to the beat.

pentameter

Pentameter, composed of lines of five
feet, has a special rhythmic feel derived
from its uneven beat. Our rhythmic instincts
favour simple repetition. Since
simplicity means two or three, or mul-
tiples thereof, five counts as difficult.

36

Music in five-time is a rarity.
Five-time is far from rare in poetry,
though, which seems strange at first: whereas the beat
of music is exact, in verse we can cheat
the rhythm, by allowing a short pause
to end each line: a comma between clauses,
as it were, to close one thought and then
begin another.

This works well with sentence
structure: attractive phrases often span
five feet; the pause suggests a sixth, so the scansion,
based on two times three, has an appealing
and intrinsically rhythmic feel.

hexameter

Hexametric lines (six feet) are rather long.
The rhymes being few, the sense of metre's not as strong
as in more compact lines.

Hexameter's far less
exciting than dimeter, say, but it expresses
big ideas in a fluent and poetic
way without the constant clash of energetic
sound-play. It's the perfect metre if your prime
concern is with the flow of words and not with rhyme.

The six feet may be subdivided into twos
and threes to add new layers of rhythm without losing
any of this metre's epic quality
or its capacity for expressivity.

heptameter

I could go on in this vein, but I have to say I am
not interested in very long, unwieldy lines. Hepta-
meter, for instance (seven feet per metric line), strikes me
as dragging its ideas out unnecessarily.
I much prefer to split it: four
feet, then a line of three
(and then a pause). That gives it more
attack and energy.

things to do

Study the metrical patterns of favourite poetry.
Which are the commonest metres? Are there any
metres you cannot find at all? Why might this be?

Practise the various metres illustrated here. Do you
agree with the author's opinions of them? Take note
of your own ideas about the relative strengths and
weaknesses of specific metres.

1e. rhyme schemes

Most of this book is made up
of pairs of lines called rhyming couplets: ⏋
line one defines the rhyme sound and the metre
which line two then follows, to complete
the pair.

A couplet's rather like

cŏuplĕt

a story boiled down to its microcosmic
essence.

🐚 The metre sets
the scene and the first rhyme word whets
our appetite.

🐚 We know the second part
is going to rhyme before we even start
to read it, and the metre tells
us when to expect the rhyme, compelling
us to read on while we try to guess
the ending.

This technique is more or less
what story-tellers use to hold
their audiences.

If we've got
a bigger story to be told,
we might prefer to use a quatrain.
That's a pair of intertwining
couplets, as I'm indicating
here, with different rhymes. The lines
most commonly use alternating
rhyme sounds.

The sense of expectation
that we feel is twice as strong,
insofar as the alternation
of the rhyme sounds means a longer
wait for matching rhymes (line three
completes the first pair; four the second).

We could go on adding more
rhyme sounds and separating pairs
of matching rhymes indefinitely,
though this is rarely as effective
as you might think. I've got four
rhymes alternating here, but there's
so much going on, it scarcely

sounds like rhyming verse
at all.

Our minds can't cope
with all those unmatched, open
rhymes. Use one or two—three,
if you must, but sparingly.

The letters on the right	A
of these lines indicate	B
rhyme sounds: A is the *ite*	A
sound, B denotes the *ate*	B
sound.	

Lettering enables
us to work with labels
to describe the rhyme scheme. That
familiar alternating pattern
is known as ABAB.
The actual rhyme sounds are not predetermined. They just happened to
be *ite* and *ate* in this case. New

rhyme sounds are given their	C
own letters as and when	D
required. The *air* and *en*	D
sounds here make up a pair	C

within a pair: CDDC.

The standard forms of poetry
with their established rhyme schemes may
be codified in this same way.

shākespeareăn
sŏnnĕt fŏrm

One of the most familiar is the sonnet:	A
a fourteen-line verse form from Italy.	B
There are two English variants, both based on	A
pentameter. This one consists of three	B
quatrains, each with new rhymes in alternating	C
rhyme pairs, ending with a rhyming couplet.	D
It's presented in two sections: eight,	C
then six lines; that's to say it's broken up	D
… at this point. Very often, the last section	E
(known as the sestet) marks a departure	F
by embarking on a new direction	E
from the thought first mooted at the start.	F
The rhyming pattern illustrated here	G
was pioneered and much used by Shakespeare.	G

miltōnĭc sŏnnĕt fōrm

A slightly later English poet, John	A
Milton, used a sonnet form with fewer	B
rhyme sounds. Whereas Shakespeare worked with two	B
rhyme words for each of seven sounds, Miltonic	A
form needs three or four rhymes based upon	A
just four or five sounds. That's a lot of true	B
rhymes for some sounds, especially since you	B
must use them meaningfully in your sonnet.	A
The opening section (which is known as the	C
octet) invariably consists of two	D
ABBA quatrains. The symmetry	C
of the sestet is slightly less strict. You	D
may use two pairs—CDCDCD—	C
or else CDECDE will do.	D

roundel

The roundel, an old French verse form, is based	A
on only two rhyme sounds: in this case *aced*	A
and *ain*. These same two sounds are heard again	B
repeatedly, but you are free to chain	B
the rhymes in any scheme that suits your taste.	A_1
One line or more is heard as a refrain,	B_1
though there's a danger this may sound inane	B
if it's a poor line. Nor should you be hasty	A
in your choice of rhyme sound: roundels mainly	B
run to fourteen lines, so you'll be faced	A
with quite a challenge trying to sustain	B
the rhymes in any scheme that suits your taste.	A_1
Of course you needn't always search in vain:	B
one line or more is heard as a refrain.	B_1

The range of possibilities
is endless, as I hope that these
few rhyme schemes illustrate.

The text I've written for them, though,
would certainly not count as poetry
(which must have greater
depth of meaning, as I will make clear
in proper detail later in this series.)

Poets that use metre
(many poets don't these days)
write lines that are complete
within themselves, so that their phrases
and their sentence structures cause
the reader of the piece to pause
at ends of lines.

Not mine. I am
inclined to make each line enjamb
into the next. Enjambment means beginning
any phrase in one line and continuing
it in the next. **enjambment**

I've found repeatedly
enjambing phrases make the metre
less important. Phrases can't be broken
up with pauses: my verse must be spoken
naturally if it's to make sense.

45

I like it when there's not much evidence
of my eccentric rhythmic work, distracting
as it may be.

Rhythm helps to activate
attention, but it's just a catalyst.

The meaning is what really matters.

Conduct some research into rhyme schemes. Analyse
the metre and rhyme schemes in a poetry anthology.
See how many different schemes you can identify. Try
to find out something about them, such as what they
are called and when and where they originated.

Select rhyme schemes that particularly interest you
and write your own verse/poetry in accordance with
their rules. Which schemes best suit your style? Why?

Invent your own metre and rhyme schemes based on
the concepts outlined in this book.

book 2:
getting better verse

book 2:
getting better verse

There's more to verse than metre
and an even beat.
Good verse is like good storytelling:
every sentence makes compelling
listening (or reading).

This
book helps you to engage your listeners'
attention every time,
not just by virtue of your rhymes
and rhythms but because you've got
a logical, well ordered plot.

2a. prōsevērse

This style of rhyming verse
is based upon a personal
belief that verse should read
as fluently as prose.

Indeed, a favourite trick of mine is to conceal the line-
breaks in my rhyming verse, so that the reader cannot
see the pattern of the verse at all. Because it looks
and reads like prose, the pauses and the phrasing tend
to sound more natural; whereas I've found that many
readers pause each time a line ends with an obvious
rhyme.

In this book, we are going to focus
on the meaning of the spoken
word. I deliberately said
the *spoken* word: verse is best read
aloud to show its full effect.

Writing verse is intellectually
more absorbing than composing
sentences in ordinary prose.
The task of matching sounds and meaning slows

the writing down, it's true, but concentrating
upon rhyme sounds helps facilitate
creative thinking, as we shall soon see.

But there's one further technicality
to be considered first.

You may
have noticed my unusual way
of rhyming, which consists of choosing
just one syllable to use
as my rhyme sound. It may be in the middle
of a word.

That's what I call a hidden
rhyme. It may not be apparent
to the ear or eye.

As far
as I'm concerned, that's good. Technique's
important, but the words must speak
as clearly as if they were not
in verse.

This is enjambment taken
one stage further, with lines breaking
not just in mid-phrase but mid-word.

Proseverse freely skates upon a grid
of mathematical exactitude

with ease, avoiding any hint of crude,
forced rhymes: such perverse phraseology
as finishes with words that first should be !

It's skilled and disciplined, but open-ended
too, such that you're able to extend
the canvas of your creativity
to capture the full breadth of your ideas,
in language brightly coloured and inventive
that keeps your readers happily attentive.

things to do

Review the text of this chapter, marking out the
rhyming syllables in each couplet (including the
passage that looks like prose but isn't). Notice how
frequently the author rhymes single syllables without
rhyming the remaining syllables of the same word.

Practise writing sentences that read like prose but that
are strictly metred, using patterns of stressed and
unstressed syllables and maybe also rhymes.

2b. getting started

Enough of technicalities!
Let's make some verse.

Perhaps the easiest
way to start is just to write
a sentence and see where it might
lead:

There's a sound of breaking glass.

I like
that.

- It grabs the attention with a striking
  image
- and it makes the reader
  wonder where it's going to lead.

And that's precisely what we need.

There's a sound of breaking glass. The children
freeze.

That's also very good. We're still
on the right track.

We've got some characters.
Who are these children? Are
they misbehaving? Has someone
been hurt?

spontaneity

A large part of the fun
of writing in this unplanned way
is never knowing what you'll say
next.

If this were to be an improvised
performance, I would be as much surprised
by my spontaneous ideas
as my audience would be.
I'd give my creativity
full vent and let my audience guide
me: their reactions would decide
how I'd proceed and when I ought to end.

The work of writing verse, though, does not lend
itself to such free-wheeling. Only nine

words in, I must decide how long the lines
will be and how I'm going to organise
the rhymes.

organisation

In short, I need to analyse
my sentences extremely carefully,
not just in terms of sense, but rhyme and metre
too. Although I can't proceed
at even one tenth of the speed
of an impromptu storyteller,
I can ensure that every element
of my work is correctly
placed for optimal effect.

There's a sound of breaking glass. The children
freeze.

I must say I don't think it will
work after all.

I wanted the enjambment:
that's what prompted me to use pentameter.

It's got too slow a beat.

Perhaps I ought to try trimeter?
That should help ensure
the pace is fast and furious.

And I don't think the present tense
sounds right. In storytelling it's more sensible
to use the past tense: this
enables greater authenticity,
insofar as invented action
may be told convincingly as fact,
while present action must be seen
to be believed.

Best make a clean
start.

A crash. A shower of shattering
glass. The (*something*) batsman …

pace

I prefer that style: the rapid
pace, short phrases. Things are happening
already. The trimeter's
working well and I've completed
my first couplet—almost.

That
rhyme's worth a mention, too: the *at*
sound hidden in the enjambing syllables.
For me at least, the thrill
of writing verse lies largely in
the rhyming.

58

Rhyming sounds are finishing
points, but they're new beginnings
too: I had to find an *at*
rhyme to complete the pair, but *batsman*
starts a new idea: it
was probably a ball that hit
the glass and smashed it. Having found
a reasonable rhyming sound,
I've also focused on the reason
for the smash.

rhymes
spark
new ideas

I guess that he's
unlikely to win praise for breaking
glass, so what next? Will he make
a run for it or stay and face
the music?

I don't want the pace
to slacken yet. My opening
idea's good, but I must bring
my readers with me, make them read
on. If my batsman just agreed
to pay the cost of the repair,
that would be dull—worthy and fair
maybe, but dull.

Much better to have conflict.
That's what keeps the readers reading on.

conflict

59

Readers love the clash of personalities
and the perverse
behaviour that derives from thwarted
aspirations.

The important
thing, though, from a purely technical
perspective, is that equilibrium
and conflict cannot co-exist.

Since equilibrium means going
nowhere, it's the enemy
of storytelling. Harmony,
peace, concord, lovely as they are,
won't do. We need events and characters
that do *more* than exist.

Conflict is the catalyst   **change**
for change—change, the kinetic force,
the electricity that courses
through the veins of every vibrant plot.

Back to our verse. Let's see how far we've got.

A cr$\overset{1}{a}$sh. A sh$\overset{2}{o}$wer of sh$\overset{3}{a}$ttering
gl$\overset{1}{a}$ss. (*Words missing*) b$\overset{3}{a}$tsman ...

The story-line's wide open still
and I could change the rhyming syllable.

In fact, I think I will.

A crash. A shower of shattering
glass. A scream. A patte-
ring of tiny feet.

I'm sticking with trimeter,
by the way. The *ing*
sound is the opening
beat of the third line.

Note how that
extremely small change—*pattering*—
transforms the story utterly,
and adds a sense of mystery.

That's sure to keep my readers guessing.

And there's no enjambment pressing
on to the fourth line.
I'll take it as a sign:
rhyme, then full stop suggests that that
first section is complete.

... A pattering
of tiny feet.
One eye half opened. Street lamps
still on. Back to sleep.

Now this
is really good: a double mystery.

I want to know

   what's meant
   by all the sounds, and

   the identity
   of the half-sleeping person,

and all because the rhyming verse
is giving shape to my ideas.

Let's look at that person. He
(or she?) can tell that it's still night-
time since the street lamps are alight.

Did he not pull the curtains? Why
not?

Maybe she's too poor to buy
such things?

Perhaps he's sleeping rough?

The noises we heard weren't enough
to rouse her. Should I let her sleep?
If so, I must think how to keep
my readers hooked.

Wake him, I say!
Let's see what part he's got to play.

A rhyme for *sleep*—*heap*? *keeping*?
people?...

    ... Băck to slĕep.
Wait! Brĕathing—sŏmeone crĕeping
ŭp. Awăke now, wăiting.
Ēyes closed, cŏncentrăting
ŏn the sŏund. Hold stĕady—
pĕnknife ăt the rĕady.
Cŏld hand—gŏing thrŏugh
my pŏckets.

Gŏtcha!

Yŏu?

I hope you can begin to see
how much one's creativity

may be enhanced by persevering
with the techniques practised here.

From an analytical
perspective, the essential skills
include the following:

analysis and creativity

● Begin at the beginning.

● Discipline
   yourself to scrutinise each syllable
   and don't move on until
   your latest sentence is completely
   right: not just its rhymes and metre
   but its meaning first and foremost.

● Consistently review your story
   by considering the questions
   that are likely to suggest
   themselves to readers as your text
   unfolds, and then decide what's next.

things to do

Continue the verse begun in this chapter.

Develop a further passage of verse based on your own
starting point.

2c. plōt

Composing phrase by phrase
and critical appraisal
are the basic tools
for writing verse.

Such rules
are always good for localised
work—when one's focused
on a single sentence.

They're less pertinent
when it comes to determining
precisely where
the story's going. Unplanned
stories may be fun,
but only if your luck
holds.

Predetermined structures
leave much less to chance.
If you know in advance
the gist of what your characters

will do, your narrative
will be the stronger
for it.

It's not wrong
to let your stories find
their way, if you don't mind
the risk that your work may
be wasted: if you stray
into an unexciting
plot, there'll be rewriting
to be done.

You can
reduce this risk by planning
the defining features,
the essential details
of your story, and
then writing towards the planned
outcome.

plan
ahead

Most storytellers
are already well
aware of how their story's
going to end before
they start to tell it. They
reserve their spontaneity
for minor details,

working carefully
along a pre-planned route.

Perhaps the most acute
analysis of the elements
of storytelling
comes from Ancient Greece,
in Aristotle's thesis
on POETICS.

He
identifies the ingredients
that make good plot:

reversal

Aristotle
speaks of the importance
of a change of fortune
as a driving force
in drama.

When the course
of people's lives is radically
altered—from bad
to good, from rich to poor,
and so on—they are surely
at their most exciting:

that is, from the writer's
point of view.

Reversal
breaks the mould of personal
experience: Will success
bring untold happiness?
How will our hero cope
when everything he'd hoped
and planned for is frustrated
by a twist of fate?

When characters are forced
to change, their true resourcefulness
is put to the test.
This is one of the best
ways that your readership
may be held in your grip.

The hero's helpless plight
subconsciously invites
their empathy such that they see
themselves in his adversity,
and likewise they identify
with him in his great hour of triumph.

discovery

Another element
of skilful storytelling
is discovery.

What Aristotle
tells us is that characters'
behaviour often changes when
they gain new information. This is beneficial
insofar as change of any
kind is a kinetic
force.

There's empathetic
power too in discovery.
The moment of
discovery is experienced
by all: not merely
by the character
but equally, concurrently
by the readers. They are there
with her in thought and spirit, sharing
in the new-found information,
basing their own calculations

poetics

69

on it, working out what they would do
in her place and then reading on with newly
exercised anticipation
of what's going to happen.

complication
and catastrophe

Events,
I think it's sometimes said, are sent
to try us. Our plans rarely
play out as they were
intended to.

So, not surprisingly,
we tend to empathise
with characters who suffer setbacks.

Complications have kinetic
energy as well.

As far as storytellers
are concerned, such setbacks are
a very useful source of narrative
digression. The achievement

aristotle's

is a great deal more believable
if the hero faces complications
and recovers from
them, in which case the audience
appreciates the rising tension
as the hero narrowly
avoids complete catastrophe.

resolution

There must be
some sort of end, of course: a resolution.

Aristotle says
that all the loose threads must be tied
up if we're to be satisfied
as readers.

This is probably
the hardest job
of writing. Endings can seem trite.
There's no such thing as happy
ever after.

We need to wrap
things up convincingly so that,

poetics

at the very least, we've reached a satisfying
stage in the ongoing journey
that is life:

- perhaps another turning
  point—the characters must face
  new issues next that have no place
  in the story being told;

- perhaps the destination's
  reached and now it's time to rest.

Either way, the resolution makes
the readers feel that they can safely break
away for good without too many
mysteries unsolved, if any.

things to do

Return to the passage of verse you created at the end
of chapter 2b.

- Identify the elements of your writing that
  correspond to Aristotle's principles.

- Are any of Aristotle's elements missing from your
  work? Would it benefit from their inclusion?

- Can you identify any structural devices in your
  work that go beyond Aristotle's thinking?

2d. knowing when to stop

"Freewheeling", as we did in chapter 2b, helps to make things happen.

If you're supremely skilful,
there's a chance you will
freewheel your way through Aristotle's
principles until you've got
a perfect story that
will be completely satisfying
for your readers.

If
freewheeling turns to endless drifting,
though, you're lost, unless
you formulate a rescue
strategy.

It's more efficient
to consider how you wish

to end before you've gone
too far; then carry on
towards that end point.

That's how I
composed ...

the ball that bounced

Mum gave me a ball. It was fantastic.
It was made of yellowy-green plastic,
very hard,
and on the card
that came with it, the picture showed
that it bounced really high and glowed
when all the lights
were out at night.

I took it straight outside to try
to make it bounce up really high.
I threw the ball down very hard
on that big flat stone in the yard
and watched it shoot up in the air
so very high.

74

too high

I stood there staring
at it, up and up and on
up to the clouds, till it was gone
from sight.

It never reappeared.
I stared on. An enormous teardrop
trickled down my nose. I went inside
and lay down on my bed and cried and cried
myself asleep.

Then someone seemed to stroke
my cheek, and it was dark, and I awoke.
I thought I heard a voice inside my head
that seemed to say "Get up. Get out of bed.
Go over to the window. There's no need to cry."
And there was my ball, bright and shining—in the sky.

75

In fact the end point was in place
before I started, in this case:
the moon might be a ball
that bounced too high. That's all
I needed.

start with
the end

There must be someone
to bounce the ball. It might be done
by somebody naive:
I could make that believable.

A child, then, would narrate
the story.

Next I concentrated
on the plot. The key
ingredients would be:

sketch
the plot

- *the new ball disappears,*

- *the child is left in tears,*

- *cries him/herself to sleep,*

- *then sees
  the moon.*

From this point, it was easy
to complete the drafting.

It was not till afterwards
that I considered what

76

use I had made of Aristotle's
teaching. I just knew immediately
that I didn't need
to worry on that score.

remember
aristotle

However, if my story
had been less assured, I might
have made the telling more exciting
by adding new discoveries,
reversals and catastrophes.

Each of these elements
is fully represented
in *The Ball that Bounced Too High*.

If I were going to justify
a somewhat longer version of
the story, I'd need more discoveries,
etc.

This loss—the ball—was catastrophic
enough in its context,
but insufficiently complex
to make a credible short story.

Had the child lost something more
significant, a parent
for example, there
would be a bigger story to

be told, with very many new
discoveries and complications.
The child's domestic situation
would be utterly
transformed—security
forgone.

This plot, with all its complex stages
might be sustained for several hundred pages.

things to do

Identify all occurrences of the Aristotelian elements
of reversal, discovery, complication, catastrophe and
resolution in *The Ball that Bounced Too High*.

Try to lengthen the story by adding new elements but
without changing the resolution, always bearing in
mind the need to hold the readers' attention. Are
there any limits to such additions?

Devise a "bigger" resolution as suggested in the
closing lines of this chapter, and sketch the plot in
outline as illustrated on page 76. Notice how the
scope for development of the idea expands
accordingly.

book 3:

constructive induction

book 3:

constructive induction

All writing, whether it serves to explain,
to make you think, or just to entertain,
is based on logic.

I will show you how
you can unleash immense creative power
with the help of two astonishingly
simple principles of reasoning:

- inductive thinking generates ideas
  and develops them creatively;

- deductive thinking takes us from profusion
  of ideas towards a firm conclusion.

3a. thōught

We think of creativity
as something of a mystery,
and rightly so. Ideas seem
to drift through some subconscious dreamworld
into the foreground of the
imagination and, if we
don't capture them at once, they're gone
into forlorn oblivion.

Does this mean that creative
people have to wait
in hope for inspiration?
Not at all. One's patience
would be sorely tested.

Many say their best
ideas have come to
them like bolts from the blue.
As far as I'm concerned,
such moments must be earned.
We need to exercise
our minds, to energise

our thoughts, to drive the process
of creation, so
that when that big idea
comes to us, we'll be
sufficiently aware
of why it's good and where
it might lead, and be skilled
enough to shape it, build
upon it and express it clearly.

In my work, I find that nearly
all of my ideas, far
from coming out of nowhere, are
occasioned by my efforts to
solve problems or discover new
perspectives on familiar themes.

Ideas, in other words, like dreams,
emerge from the subconscious.

Thoughts
occur when memories are brought
out of their idle store and exercised
within the new context
of present issues:

memories and the subconscious

* In a nightmare,
  our subconscious fears excite

85

remembered images that feed our sense of fear.

* When we are reading something, we subconsciously delve deep into our memory for images that bring the text to life.

* When there is a perplexing problem to be solved, we scour our memories to see if our experience has anything to offer.

It's this processing
of memories—signs, symbols,
sounds, smells, textures, images—
that we call thought:
when memories are brought
together with, maybe,
external stimuli.

external
stimuli

Some text, a conversation,
a tricky situation:
these become ingredients
that our minds knead
into a yeasty dough
that we may choose to throw
away or set to rise.

Every batch comprises
an unprecedented
mix of things—events,
thoughts, feelings—because these
specific memories
are ours alone.

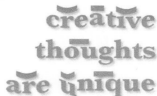

Potentially
at least, the dough is an idea.
It's potential will not be
fulfilled unless we have the will
and, as importantly, the skill
to cut and shape it as it rises
and bake it into appetising
food for thought: for us, or to
be shared with others, to make new
ideas.

Everyone has the
ingredients to make the yeasty
mix. In that sense we are all
creative. But that's just the smallest
part of it.

It is the will
and skill and, through them, the fulfilment
that distinguish poets, painters,
sculptors, writers from the main

stream of humanity. The fashioning
of raw ideas, the passion
you feel for expressing them;
these, with your exclusive memories
and motivations make
you stand out as an expert baker:
one of many, yet unique.
For no one else can truly speak
as you speak, write as you write.

You
must first, though, like the dough, be proven.
Thinking's just the start of it.
The difficult bit is committing
thoughts to written text.

So when
that next idea comes, grab your pen
at once, and don't let go again.

things to do

Study your own thought processes. When you next
begin a train of thought, try to list the memories that
spring to mind. Identify their contributions to the
development of your ideas, or the extent to which
they motivate you to take action.

3b. creativity

Aristotle offers
further relevant guidance
in his philosophical
essays.

Besides
the elements of plot,
he also identified
the rules for logic.

What
he teaches us is that
our seemingly chaotic
thoughts fall into patterns.
These inspire creative,
often enigmatic
leaps that elevate
mere thoughts into conclusive
arguments that state
our point of view, inducing
others to react
to it.

He most usefully
provides us with a practical
process for reasoning
that works exactly
as our minds work. The
essential feature is that when
we pick up two or three
or more perceptions—pictures, sentences
and so on—we instinctively
evaluate them, blending
them into one thought that links
them up somehow. This processing
is what we call "inductive thinking"
or "inductive reasoning".

inductive reasoning

Let's give it a try. I'll write
some sentences and try to bring
them into one new thought.

* Last night,
  Joe dreamt he was a lion-tamer,
  and a lion tried to bite
  him.

propositions

* When Joe was small, and Grandma came
  to visit with her silvery
  grey cat, Joe always vanished, claiming
  to be ill.

Subconsciously
our minds start working to assemble
a coherent picture. We
try to construct it from remembered
pictures, sounds, emotions—lions,
childhood days. We may feel empathy
for Joe.

gaps

We can't help trying
to fill in the gaps by posing
questions—*How old is Joe? Why
this fear of cats? What's meant by Joe's
dream?*—and inventing answers—*He's
much older now; Perhaps he's chosen
to confront his fear; Perhaps the reason
for it is some formative
event in infancy.* All these
are just subjective guesses, driven
by our own unique experiences.

questions

hypotheses

Notice how they give
us further food for thought. Joe's fear
has now become a burning issue
in our minds.

Were we to hear
more facts about Joe's life, the mystery
might soon be solved.

If not,
the only answers come by listening
to our thoughts.

This, then, is what
inductive reasoning is:

- taking
  thoughts and observations,

- slotting
  them together somehow,

- making
  new thoughts,

- drawing hypothetical
  conclusions from them,

- breaking
  new creative ground.

It's letting
your creative instincts lead
you where they will.

Once it is set
in train, inductive thinking feeds
upon itself: it is an endless
process.

The creative freedom
that it offers us extends
through the domain of memory
towards the ungoverned splendours
lurking in the infinity
of our ineffable imagination.
That's why creativity
knows no bounds and no limitations.

things to do

Continue the process of inductive reasoning about Joe, as follows:

- Identify a theme or themes that are shared by the two propositions on page 90.

- Invent further propositions along similar lines.

- Draw hypothetical conclusions based on the extended set of propositions.

Begin a train of inductive thought by focusing on a specific memory or observation, and allow your mind to work freely upon it, taking note of thoughts as they occur to you. Do not interrupt until you have collected sufficient results to compare your thought processes with those described here.

3c. ănalȳsīs

Inductive thinking's strength lies in
the way it thrives on accidental
and undisciplined
connections, but it lacks
the power to persuade.

It widens
our creative range
without requiring us to tidy
up our thoughts. The danger
is that our creative instincts
cannot be relied
upon to furnish a convincing
argument.

Deciding
which of several directions
we should take is not
creative; nor is the selection
of thoughts that fit the plot
we're working on. The output of
each session of inductive

thinking must be garnered, governed,
cut back and constructed
into a coherent line
of careful thought, that tells
some sort of story with a final
outcome, and compels
the reader/listener.

Having thrown
wide the creative doors,
we need to shut them and take ownership
of one or more
ideas that stand out, abandoning
the rest.

focused
thinking

We need
to change our mind-set into analytical
mode, leading
our thoughts rather than being led
by them, and narrowing
them to a well drawn line instead
of idly broadening
them out.

I've chosen that word idly
quite deliberately.
Instinct leads the creative side
of things; the analytical

95

bit is more skilled by far,
and not at all spontaneous.
Once more, let's look to Aristotle
to explain.

Deductive thinking is the drawing
of definite, immovable
conclusions: it's what lawyers
have to do: to prove
things beyond reasonable doubt.

I'll try to illustrate,
beginning, this time, with the outcome:

*Joe has an innate
fear of all cats.*

The fact that Joe
would always hide from Grandma's
cats might well be used to show
that his is a long-standing
fear. That doesn't make the fear
innate, though.

If, however,
we had evidence that clearly
showed that *Joe had never
been attacked or threatened by*

his Grandma's cats and we
could somehow furnish a reliable
and fully detailed
record of Joe's every influence
before the cats
first visited, we might begin
to prove for certain that
Joe's fear was in his nature, not
his nurture.

Proving even
so much, then, would take a lot
of work.

beyond
reasonable
doubt

But how could we
hope to establish beyond reasonable
doubt that Joe
feared all cats: panthers, Siamese
cats, pumas, Maine Coons, ocelots,
Exotic Short Hairs, cheetahs,
Russian Blues and more?

We'd need to draw up a complete
list and go on to explore
Joe's feelings towards every cat
that ever was.

If there
were any single feline that

97

he feared not, our precarious
argument would fall.

The burden
of proof is too great
because I chose to use the word
all. If, instead, I'd stated
simply that Joe was afraid
of cats—much less precise—
the proof of it would have been made
far simpler:

*Joe loves ice
cream.*

facts

Grandma's cats are harmless creatures.

*Sometimes, when Joe's Grandma
offers Joe ice cream to eat,
provided he will stand
still for five minutes while her two
cats come and lick his toes,
Joe looks most anxious and refuses.*

We deduce that *Joe's
afraid of cats.*

conclusion

It's still not quite
right. Some more facts are needed
for it to be watertight
(Perhaps Joe's disobedient,
not fearful).

It will do
for now, though.

The important
thing is how it leads us through
the facts, along the shortest
route to a persuasive, credible
interpretation
of them.

We are being led   **leading on**
towards a destination
by manipulative distillation
of the facts.

If we accept the truth of this
conclusion—that Joe acts
as he does out of fear—Joe's fear
becomes a fact that may
be used deductively to steer
us further along the way
of logical extrusion
towards some grand conclusion.

99

things to do

The conclusion (on page 98) that Joe is afraid of cats is not fully supported by the facts. Review the supporting logic and:

- add/amend "facts" with the aim of proving beyond reasonable doubt that Joe is afraid of cats;

- draw alternative deductive conclusions based on the facts (adding/amending as appropriate).

Create further conclusions about Joe and link them with the "fear" conclusion deductively to arrive at a "grand" conclusion.

Study others' work for evidence of deductive thinking. For example, detective novels and analytical newspaper articles are fundamentally deductive. Identify the deductive outcome and the facts or premises that underpin it. Has the writer proven his/her case beyond reasonable doubt? How could the logic be strengthened?

Develop your own deductive arguments, beginning with inductive reasoning.

3d. creative writing

Inductive and deductive reasoning
are inextricably
connected.

- Without free
  association of ideas,
  there would be no progress,
  no new thinking, no
  new writing.

- Without narrowing
  our field of thought and bringing
  it towards a thought-provoking
  end, our minds would be a mass of broken,
  unconnected, unintelligible
  loose ends, meaningless and glib.

Creative writing, in this sense,
is a misnomer: the inconsequential
nature of creative thinking sees
to that. Inductive reasoning
must have its day, of course,

but it's no use until it is endorsed
by critical evaluation
and meaningful interpretation.

Let me show you how it works in practice
by embarking on some actual
creative writing.

I'll try some inductive
thinking and, with any luck,
I'll hit on something useful.

⊙   There's a sign
that says *To Let*.

    Another fine
Spring day: Amanda takes her children
to the park.

    I want my Daddy.

    Still no message: what's become of him?

**random
images**

The first of these were random images:
the sign; the outing to the park.

The image of the children was the spark
for the induction to begin:
the sign is on their house; they're in
the throes of moving house.

102

How old
are the children? There's an infant holding
back her tears.

She wants her Daddy.
That's it! That's why she's so sad.
He's obviously left home recently.
Amanda's wondering why he
has failed to get in touch.

- An accident,
  perhaps?

- Maybe he meant
  to disappear?

**unbroken
train of
thought ...**

This train
of thought takes longer to explain
than it took to occur. Inductive thinking
happens in the blinking
of an eye.

That's not surprising
if you only realise
how used we are to making sense
of information that's immensely
complex.

When our senses fill
with sights, sounds, smells all unfamiliar,

103

we interpret them at lightning
speed.

So it is quite
an easy matter to
interpret just a few
words.

They're the tiny sketch
that we, by instinct, stretch
across the panoramic
canvas
of the imagination, upon which
our memory paints a richly
textured, colourful invention:
living, breathing, three-dimensional.

All this unbidden and, perhaps,
without our even knowing that we're tapping
into what may prove to be
a truly great idea.

... serial
induction

I call this process serial induction.
Ideas are hurled like stucco
onto an empty wall without regard
to how intelligent they are.

Deductive thinking punctuates
or even punctures the creative

seam by challenging
or questioning
its output.

Going back to poor
Amanda: we were still not sure
what happened to her man.

Was there an accident, or did he plan
to go, or was it both these things
or something else?

deductive
pause

This question brings
the inductive thinking to a halt while we
deduce which path is best and cite the reasons
for our choice.

In a creative setting
such as this, we may let imagination be our guide:
some more induction; then decide.

- Paul lies unconscious in intensive care.
- For two whole days, Amanda's unaware
  of where he's got to.
- Their
  young daughter takes it badly and falls ill.
- The phone's cut off: they couldn't pay the bill.

Or I might focus on the planned abandonment:

- As he speeds towards the ferry,
  Roger feels a terrible
  pang of remorse.

- Perhaps he should
  have said where he was going? But he couldn't
  bring himself.

- She deserved no better,
  but the twins?

- Too bad. He had to get away.

I call this parallel
induction: telling
different stories
from the same point, to explore
alternative ideas creatively.

Though these ideas emanate
from a single source, they're quite distinct.
They might conceivably be linked
together, or I might reject
one; I might make some more, select
a few that suit my style and then connect
them, with the help of more

induction, into a coherent story.
The deductive element is fairly
slight so far. It's merely choosing
which inductive train of thought to use.

But if we punctuate the thought process
by posing searching, fundamental questions—
such as *Where is all this leading?* or
What am I trying to say?—by thinking forward
to the outcome, we provide
a focal point towards which we may guide
our thoughts.

structural deduction

It seems to me that those
parallel scenarios
suggest a theme of reconciliation,
with which both ideas are connected:

- Andrew, disillusioned, runs away
  from wife and family, but doesn't say
  where he is going or why.

- Amanda, searching for him, finds him lying
  half-dead in the wreckage of his car
  and saves his life.

- They realise how fortunate they are
  to have each other.

107

Suddenly I've got
an interesting plot
in outline.

If it seems
familiar, it's because the theme's
as old as humankind.
That's not to say that I won't find
new angles, though, for what
I must do next is to flesh out my plot
inductively and, since I'm writing fiction,
my field of thought is unrestricted:
if my imagination can conceive
it and my readers will believe
in it, it will be valid.

I
must simply work out all the reasons why
the reconciliation
happens and explain the situation
step by step.

Alternatively
I might merely give
some tantalising clues
so that my readers have to use
their own imagination to explain
my meaning.

108

This deductive train
of thought is the defining
moment. I can now design
my plot with confidence. I may
include my first ideas or throw them all away,
as long as I am mindful
of the need to find
inductive story lines that fit
my purpose, and produce my written
text accordingly.

things to do

Experiment with the techniques outlined in this chapter by pausing the *Amanda* story and applying your own inductive and deductive processes.

Give free rein to your inductive thinking, so that you move far away from the author's initial ideas. Then, starting with your own materials, practise:

- using parallel induction as a means of deciding which path(s) to follow;

- establishing an interesting deductive conclusion and working towards it.

amanda

It was a long wait. She
stayed by the bed where he
lay silent in a coma.
She would not go home,
she told herself, until—
she knew not what.

The stillness
was unbearable.
Why did he go? Why did
he not say where?

The lid
of one eye flickered open,
then the other. Hope
was born again.

He scanned
the room. She placed her hand
on his and smiled. Her eyes
met his.

She recognised
that look—of fear and hatred—
and she knew, too late,
that all the promises he'd made
were lies, and that she was betrayed.

110

book 4:
stirring words

book 4:

stirring words

I'd like to focus our
attention on the power
of language.

Simple words and phrases,
well used, can have an amazing
impact on the people who
are listening or reading. Do
you ever wonder
how it's done?

I've got some useful principles
to show you in
these pages—to help you use exciting
words and phrases in your writing.

4a. ĕvōcătĭve language

The signals we receive
by way of hearing, touch, taste, sight and smell
are keys to the complex retrieval
system of the mind, compelling
memories to spring
from sleep into the elevated
realm of reasoning.

For instance, when someone gives us a plate
of food, we cannot help

- remembering
  shapes, colours, textures, smells,

- relating
  past meals to the present
  one,

- evaluating
  this meal's strengths and weaknesses,

116

- identifying various ingredients

- and drawing wider inferences.

We might recall the time when we'd
last eaten fresh asparagus,
and this might lead
our thoughts away into some far-off
time and place in deepest memory.

Such reasoning is even more remarkable
when all our energy
is focused on the written
word: when all we see
are symbols.

symbols
unlock
memories

Just one little
word is all it takes to spark immensely
complex trains of thought, as intricate
as it might be if all our senses
were at work.

In fact,
we think the more intensely
when there's nothing to distract
us from the task of thinking. Furthermore,
because our minds are not forced to react
to what's now happening in the story
of our lives, we're free

117

to focus on exploring
our own selves: our memory
provides the characters and sets the scene.

When we are reading, all our energy
is concentrated on the screen
of our mind's eye, on building
pictures, finding meanings
within the receptacle
of living memory.

This processing
of half-forgotten data is the thrill
of reading. By interpreting
through the kaleidoscope
of memory we bring
to simple text a cornucopia
of personal experience
that brings the words to life for us and opens
pathways into the dimension
of the imagination.

**all language
is evocative**

In short, we make sense
of insufficient information
by calling up remembered sensory
perceptions: that's to say by evocation.

All language may be said to be
evocative through its

118

symbolic nature. Even
the most incidental little
words like *and* evoke some memories,
such as the codes we use to translate written
symbols into sounds and feasible
interpretations.

ĕvōcătĭve
soūnds

Sound and sense are the keys
to higher forms of evocation.

For example, when we hear an *ell*
sound without any further information
as to its meaning, it may well
evoke for us the gentle
tolling of a bell.

Or if we read the word *descent*,
we may remember cycling down a hill
at breakneck speed, or trying to document
our family tree.

As our minds fill
with memories, we may
experience the thrill
of real emotions. We replay
the scene and, if the memory is vivid,
feel at least an echo of the way
we must have felt when we were living
it: joy, thirst, hope, fear...

ărōusĭng
ĕmōtĭons

119

The most evocative
words, then, connect with our experience
and our emotions, bringing them
out of the distant past into the here
and now. If we allow
it, these thoughts will initiate
their own inductive reasoning
process; such is the creative
power of stirring words.

things to do

Select a piece of text that strikes you as evocative.

Analyse its language, highlighting words and phrases
that are particularly stimulating to your mind.
Analyse your response to some of these, taking note
of the images and other sensations evoked by the text
and, if appropriate, the inductive process whereby one
evoked memory leads to another.

Contrast this with a relatively "dull" piece of writing
that seems to have little or no evocative power.

What are the criteria that set truly evocative language
apart from the rest?

4b. ambiguity

The power of language to evoke compelling
images is at its greatest
when there is some element
of ambiguity in (latent)
meaning.

Take a word like *knot*,
for instance. You can't say
with any certainty precisely what
it means, unless I point the way
towards one of its copious
meanings:

- nautical miles per hour;

- an obligation;

- a tangle in a rope;

- a hill;

- a complex problem;

- an Arctic-breeding sandpiper;

- a condition;

- a binding;

- a carved knob;

- a growth in human tissue;

and more besides.

Were I to say *the river
pirates sped off at a rate
of knots*, you wouldn't give
much thought to that word *knots*:
your mind goes straight
to the specific nautical
interpretation.

Also,
knots is one of the more trivial
words here. Its power to enthral
might well be cast much wider
by making it the focus of attention
and, importantly, by hiding
the precise dimensions
of its meaning. For example:

> There
> it was: the knot, the very knot
> itself, that had been staring
> at him all these months.

diverse
meanings

context
creates
ambiguity

We can't say what
that means with any certainty.

Our instinct is to guess.
We search for knots within our memory
and, if there's time for a full investigation,
we will find
associations for each of the different
sorts of knot that come to mind.

This much more non-specific
introduction to *the knot* imposes
almost no constraints. It might
bear any one of those
interpretations: obvious or quite
obscure. And so its power to
evoke is made the greater
by broadening its scope for ambiguity.

ălternătĭve
mēanĭngs
ĕnhănce
ĕvŏcătĭon

Whilst that scope emanates
primarily from focused
dictionary definitions, it
need not end there.

Our minds evoke
associatively, flitting
freely from idea to idea
and collecting memories
along the way.

123

If we
take time to stop and think, our minds may seize
on unforeseen associations
(by inductive reasoning).

When we read, our imaginations
range less freely, insofar
as we are being directed
by the text we see. And yet we are
associative: the unexpected
happens anyway,
particularly when the writer brings
symbolic meanings into play.

Metaphor's a singularly
powerful associative
tool. Ideas serve as symbols
for others that aren't stated
in the text.

metaphor

The prehistoric images
carved on cave walls suggest
that metaphor's as old
as thought itself. The scenes of life expressed
in them are longer stories told
through symbols: crude lines etched
in stone evoke remembered images
in our mind's eye; a single sketch

symbolic
meaning

124

becomes a living, present,
detailed picture.

This example illustrates
symbolic thinking fairly
clearly. Literally
speaking, metaphor means

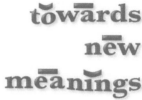

- upward bearing,

- carrying beyond.

A metaphor
invites us to
interpret words beyond the usual set
of meanings, making us construe
new, plausible alternatives.

The thought process is fundamentally
inductive, although there's a further, salient,
deductive aspect. This is best explained
through an example.

Let's consider
that word *knot* again.

It has its origins in Dutch, High Middle
German and Old English. The
essential themes are rope
and intertwining,

and the O.E.D.
shows how most other meanings opened
up around the central
principle.

- The knot of hard, contracted
  rope, in Middle English, lent
  its name to a compacted
  lump of human tissue and, at more
  or less the same time, to a complication
  in a story.

- The nautical knot, too, is taken from
  a length of rope with evenly
  positioned knots: the speed
  of any vessel travelling at sea
  could be precisely gauged by feeding
  out the rope and taking
  note of the rate of knots.

This sense of knots
as lumps or marks that serve as break-points
in a line or plot
continues to develop to this day,
through *node*: directly from the Latin
nodus (*knot*) by way
of Middle English (*tumour*).

meaning
evolves
inductively

126

Mathematically
speaking, *node* means *junction*,
intersection. Scientists
have taken up this theme and hung
new meanings on it, often highly
specialised.

Such etymology
is evidence of the
inductive power of language: letting
words evolve through free
association of ideas.

There's
a metaphorical dimension
too:

- all these knots were
  derived, by simple logical extension,
  from the knotted rope;

- the fundamental
  rope knot may
  stand as a metaphor for any one
  of them—most of them, anyway.

I know that I can open
up some of these possibilities
in readers' minds with the appropriate
symbolic keys.

Back to my previous example:

> There
> it was: the knot, the very knot
> itself, that had been staring
> at him all these months, so small a dot
> upon the blood-stained chart of his
> forlorn adventure, yet
> so raw, so swollen, as if all his misery
> were pent up in the unsettled
> tangle of its coils.

Consider what I've done here. This is no
mere knot. This is emotion boiling
up to an explosive
climax.

I've put all the emphasis
upon the metaphor. Note in
particular the visceral
words: *blood-stained*, *swollen*, *raw*.

My principal
concern is to convey
a physical sensation
of discomfort, which I do by playing
up to your imagination.

ĕmōtĭonăl ēvŏcatĭon

128

This knot is a tumour
of distressed anxiety, and yet
it's more than that. There's lots of room
for doubt. The central metaphor
holds out the possibility
that this knot is an intellectual
problem too, so grievous
as to have a most profound effect
upon our hero.

associative thinking

Lastly, since
I want to make you think
associative thoughts, I add some incidental
elements that link
up with another knot
or two:

- the tangled cords suggest a rope,
- and there's the image of the dot
  upon a chart.

I'm hoping
that a few of my readers may connect
with nodes as knots, though that
may be too indirect
for most.

Such minor details do not matter
greatly. What's important is

129

the powerful evocative
potential of the metaphorical
construction. By unlocking
memories across
a spectrum of symbolic meanings, we
create an image rich with possibilities
of meaning,
and use deductive thinking to identify
precisely what the writer meant.

things to do

Continue the illustrative text about the knot,
extending the metaphor into new areas of narrative.

Browse through your dictionary, looking for words
with many meanings. Consider the extent to which
such words are intrinsically metaphorical. Choose
some favourites and devise metaphors based on them.
Bearing in mind the pattern of development of
meanings for your chosen words, try to imagine ways
in which they may develop further in the future.

Consider other associative devices such as simile and
onomatopoeia. Explain how they help to make
language more evocative, in terms of symbolism,
associative thinking and inductive reasoning.

130

4c. persistence

Our minds work at amazing
speed. We read a word or phrase
and instantly
we see
an image out of memory.

Good writers and good story-tellers
skilfully develop
that first picture
by evoking many more in quick
succession.

Most information makes a fairly faint impression
on us, though.
Thoughts come and go
amid the ebb and flow
of information.

When we're making friendly conversation,
it's usually ephemeral
and, therefore, rarely memorable.

But even
if we try to hold on to the details
in our mind,
they are not always easily consigned
to memory.

memorability

Whilst this
is by no means a simple issue,
the logistics
of it may be factored in simplistic
terms of:

- the information's
  grip on the imagination,

- and the speed
  at which the information strikes the reader
  or listener.

The attention factor's
key. Text must impact
on our imagination in some way
if we're to stay
attentive.
We must always give our readers some incentive
to keep reading on.

The rate
at which our minds collate

the data is important too, because
it's in the pauses
that the processing of memories is done.

Our understanding
is impaired if we don't give
evocative
words time to act as keys
to thought-provoking memories.
A good idea's wasted
if it's instantly displaced
by something else.

Of course our readers
read at any speed
they please.
Such subtleties
as metaphor can all too easily
go flying past
unseen if we read on too fast.

As writers we should not assume we can dictate
the rate
our text is to be read.
We need to concentrate instead
on keeping hold of the
attention of the most cursory
of readers: building up our imagery

133

and our symbols
gradually, gently but persistently
enlisting
the support of the
imagination.

Note the key
word here: *persistently*.

persistence

1: determined
effort

I dare
say that you could infer
correctly what persistence meant
in the context of that sentence:
firm, or maybe even obstinate, continuance
in
the face
of hasty
reading. That's *persistence* in its basic
meaning.

I have chosen
it because it's one of those
intrinsically metaphorical
words which, furthermore,
through its generic sense, provides the spark
for two remarkable,
superbly apt
new metaphors to guide this chapter.

The moving images we see
in film or on TV
are made extremely realistic
by optical persistence.

2: optical persistence

If we stare
at something bright and clear—a yellow square,
say, on a red background—then shut our eyes,
the image dies
away, of course, but not immediately.
What we are seeing
is a persistent image on the retina.

We get
the same effect with any image, though
most are not so
persistent—a mere fraction
of a second—but the fact
of this persistence means that pictures
flashed on screen in quick
succession linger
long enough to seem to intermingle,
causing the fluidity
through which we think we see
continuous movement.

Consider how this might apply
in terms of the mind's eye:

135

the retina of the
imagination. Here we see
remembered images, evoked
by sounds, smells, tastes, the spoken
word, and so
on. Such images are relatively slow
to fade, especially
if those initial thoughts are reinforced
by further memories.

To this
extent persistence,
in the mind's eye, is controllable.
The writer's goal
is to prolong it.

My
next metaphor comes from the science
of ecology.

3: ecological persistence

A chemical is said to be
persistent if it lasts
in the environment long past
the time when it was introduced—not merely
seconds, but years,
decades maybe.

To me,
this symbolises memory,

where images are filed away
for future use. They may
go unobserved for years, but still
they are accessible
to the imagination
through the magic of evocation.

wrĭttĕn

The mind's eye is a sandy
beach at high tide. As we stand
on it, we dint
it, and our footmarks are precisely printed
in it. We build castles and embellish
them with shells
and stones and flags, and the idyllic
scene persists, until
a gentle wave creeps up and flattens
it—and that is that.

ĭn thĕ

sānd

ētched

Long term memory's a rocky
pool, awash with cockles
and with drifting,
shimmering seaweed. Its uncertain, shifting
population changes constantly
with tides and seasons,
wind and rain, and yet
its bedrock has been firmly set
into a most persistent
pattern of primeval history.

ŭpŏn thĕ

rōck

137

As writers, we must be
content to work with the
inconstant sand. Our castles, built of memories,
are ephemeral,
soon to be levelled
by the tide, but we can revel
in them.

We can only hope our sketches
may be etched
forever
on the bedrock of the human mind but, clever
and persistent though
we may be, we can never know
for sure.

prolonging
persistence

We can make stronger
images if we prolong
persistence in the mind's eye, hoping that this length
and strength
may bear them down and keep
them till they're rooted in the deep
recesses
of the rocky pool. But we can only guess
as to their chances of survival.

How, then, do we contrive
to write text that is truly

memorable beyond the fluid,
fleeting, shifting sands of the mind's eye?
These books are my
best answer to that penetrating
question, with its many
facets, but a little summary
will probably
be useful at this point.

As far
as I can tell, there are
two factors whereby we
can influence memorability:

- time spent assembling
  pictures in the mind's eye;

- the range of memories
  evoked.

One way
to memorise text is to say
it over and again.
Such blatant repetition plainly
will not do
from a creative writer's point of view:
one's readers would be bored
to tears.

repetition
encourages
retention

But if we do it more
discriminately and discreetly,
such as by repeating
chosen words or concepts,
the images evoked live on
much more persistently
in the mind's eye.

**firing the
imagination**

The imagery
used in this chapter,
for example, is designed to capture
your imagination
by persistent evocation.
My aim is to persuade
you, after all this text has faded
from the retina
of your mind's eye, that my two metaphors
of rock and sand
provide the keys to understanding
long and short term memory.

I have repeated the
essential
word, *persistence*, while maintaining your attention,
by encouraging you to
develop several new
associations for it. All I hope

is that I've opened
up some hidden doors
within your mind.

My metaphors,
because of their respective
ambiguities, connect
the much repeated
word with other, hitherto completely
unrelated
concepts.

forging
memorable
links

Such connections spark creative
thinking:
we remember seaside holidays, and link
them up with our
new train of thought.

For me at least, the power
of that image—
of the sand at high tide as a symbol
for the mind's eye—is compelling.
Repeatedly, I tell
myself it must not be forgotten.

To make sure it's not,
I wrote it down as soon as it first came to mind.
(I find
that writing is the surest

141

way of capturing mercurial
new thoughts persistently.)

My long term memory
has taken it on board as well,
though. That's because I tell
it in my writing classes:
all I do is think of castles
in the sand; as soon as those words are spoken,
they evoke
these metaphors to guide my speech,
enabling me to teach
without the slightest need for preparation,
from memories that fire the imagination.

Experiment with the hypothesis that evocation is facilitated by pauses. Read an evocative text aloud to some listeners without pausing. Then read the same passage again, taking care to create a short pause after every phrase. Discuss the respective effects with your audience.

Try to remember as much as possible about the text you have already read in this book. Make a list of the things that spring immediately to mind and of other associations that you remember as a result. Then look at the book again, comparing its contents with your list. What worked for you, what didn't, and why?

Intrinsically metaphorical words, such as *knot* and *persistence*, are far from rare. Browse through a dictionary and select some words with a similarly diverse range of meanings. Attempt some metaphorical writing of your own, exploiting as many as possible of the concepts discussed in this book.

book 5:

proficiency in poetry

book 5:
proficiency in poetry

Poetry and verse are not at all identical.
This text's in verse but you're not meant
to think of it as poetry. Whereas
verse is concerned with rhythm, poetry has
its roots in meaning.

In this book, I seek
to pull together all of the techniques
that I've explored so far and show how we
can write verse that is also poetry.

147

5a. what is poetry?

I can't remember ever being taught
precisely what is meant by poetry.
It is as if nobody ever thought
to tell me.

Poetry was something we
must learn to recognise by simply reading
it, or listening. Appreciation
was what mattered, so there was no need
for definition.

There were intimations
that a poem should be rhythmical,
but I found many that were not; that poetry
was always deeply meaningful,
but comic verse is rarely deep—although
anthologies of poetry include
it readily.

This inexactitude
of definition is not new. The O.E.D.

148

informs us of a Middle English
definition (obsolete), when poetry
was nothing other than the thing
we call creative writing: any text
drawn from imagination might be classed
as poetry.

A somewhat more complex
interpretation follows, one that's lasted
to this day, and forms the basis for
my teaching in this book. To me, it has
poetic resonance. I'll not re-order
its fine words, but let you read them as
I found them in my Shorter O.E.D.
and only then say what they mean to me.

⚘ Poetry:

> the expression or embodiment of beautiful or
> elevated thought, imagination or feeling, in
> language and a form adapted to stir the
> imagination and emotions.

If I were asked to sum that up in three
words, I would say that poetry is

⚘ good creative writing.

There's the recipe
for it. In my view every writer should
observe these principles in all of his
or her work, be it verse or prose or proseverse.

Stirring the imagination is
what writing's all about.

good
creative
writing

A few well chosen,
thought provoking words have more impact
on thoughtful readers than a half a ton
of empty text.

Insofar as attracting
and engaging previously uncommitted
readers is our mission, we
should always strive to write pure poetry.

There is a somewhat more prosaic element
of that same definition that
I did not quote above: a parallel
aspect of poetry as verse or patterned
language of some sort.

A somewhat tenuous
link exists between the verse and the
expressive use of language, such that any
patterned text may count as poetry
regardless of its lack of depth, while stirring

words are poetry without regard
to whether they are patterned.

This concurs
with my perception that there are no hard
and fast rules when it comes to writing poetry:
we're free to make our own: and so
I shall.

ver̄se

You may already have detected
my emphatic differentiation
between poetry and verse. Correctly
so.

ănd

pōĕtry̆

It would be an exaggeration
to claim that I am writing poetry
just now.

This is proseverse, mere mathematical
word-play. It isn't meant to be
more than a teaching aid. If there's a smattering
of poetry, it's incidental.

Poetry is for the intellect,
I think, while verse technique is fundamentally
primeval. That's why the effect
of poetry on the emotions may
be heightened by the subtle interplay
of rhymes and rhythms.

Words communicate
through memory and the imagination.

Sounds and rhythms, meanwhile, resonate
with our primordial selves. Their evocation
is not intellectual but primitive.
Their patterns have no meaning, yet
they're very much a part of the subliminal
mood music that defines poetic
language.

Meaning is the trigger that
calls up remembered images from sleep.
When meaning is enhanced by rhythmic patterns
that appeal directly to the deepest
instincts that define humanity,
it opens up our minds to poetry.

things to do

Consider some of your favourite poetry in a new light:
look through its intellectual content, as through a
window, at the primeval patterns that underpin the
meaning. To what extent do such patterns enhance
your enjoyment of the writing?

5b. sūbtēxt

How long should a poem be?

The O.E.D. gives us no guidance.
It's for the poet to decide
and there is great diversity
of views.

The most extensive poems
run to several hundred pages.
Some of them are seen as major
milestones on the map of progress,
cultural as well as literary,
down the centuries.

Conversely, poems can compress
great thoughts into a tightly fitting
pattern with just a few well reasoned
words. One of my favourites questions
our existence fundamentally
with almost terrifying
brevity.

It reads:

I.
Why? *

And most are short.

It's evident
from the abundance of anthologies
of poetry, and from
the fact that modern poets commonly
present work in slim volumes,
that poets like to work in miniature:
a page or two, or less.

If we decide to write haikus
or sonnets, say, we work within
extreme constraints: we must express
poetic thoughts, but only using
syllables that fit the chosen
pattern.

**brevity
in poetry**

Does this tendency
towards brevity in poetry
come from the fact that poetry flows
less readily onto the page
than prose?

from WORDS TO RHYME WITH by Willard Espy

154

There is some truth in that
assertion.

But, to me, what matters
most to poets is engaging
the imagination, taking
readers' thinking to a higher
level. Insofar as poetry
is capable of making
its point with a few inspiring
words, it seems to me there's no
point in prolonging it unnecessarily.

A poet ought
to concentrate on being thought-
provoking. Too much length may lessen
the effect. We make our readers
think by giving them a mystery
to solve, making them listen
to their inner voice.

**ă sēnse
ŏf mȳstĕrў**

We need
to say what must be said—no more—
and then fall silent, pass the baton
to the reader, who must run
with it. The reader must explore
for him or herself and, once that
process begins, our work is done.

A haiku here will help explain
what I am saying:

*Memories are grist
to life's philosophies here
on the mind's millstone*

My train
of thought breaks off almost too quickly,
even as it's gathering speed.
For best effect, you should stop reading,
shut your eyes and let the pictures
come to life upon the screen
of your mind's eye.

My memory
throws up an image of a recent
trip to an old mill. The scene
is set, but only partially.
My next task is to try to piece
the metaphor together.

Abstract
nouns like *memory* and *mind*
cannot be readily defined
in visual terms, so the elaboration
of the old mill image

**time
to think**

is not strictly visual
in nature.

**inductive
exploration**

- I think of the mill
  as my own head.

- The millstone symbolises
  the process of thinking
  gristful memories, translating
  them into new food for thought.

And now the only missing link
is *life's philosophies*.

Creative
thinking, I believe, when brought
to bear on the pursuit of meaning,
is philosophising by
another name.

And there is my
mind's story in the seventeen
well chosen syllables of that
haiku. If I had merely glanced
at it and then moved on, my chances
of interpreting the matter
of it would be all too slim.

I had to take my time, reflecting
on the words by reading and

re-reading them before the images
evoked could be connected
fully with my understanding.

Interpretations such as the
above are based on subtext.

Subtext is a sort of mental double
image of the text, that we
construct from memories and, being
made of memories, it is
unique to each of us.

We visualise
the text inductively
by making idiosyncratic
leaps of thought. Whereas the written
words are fixed, there is no limit
to the scope for subtext.

**subtext
is limitless**

- At

    the one extreme—the text—are little,
    faintly sketched outlines of images
    with huge gaps everywhere

- and, at the other, are elaborately
    worked out pictures, fabulously
    rich, with multifarious
    content.

158

So, when the initial
sketch consists of seventeen
syllabic strokes, the layers of meaning
it evokes into position
on the screen of the mind's eye
may be so bright and colourful
and deep that we no longer see
the words beneath.

But that is why
the poem works for us: it's pulling
gently on the strings of the
imagination.

the poetry
is in
the subtext

The work of writing
poetry is first and foremost
about subtext.

To me, the more
scope for subtext, the more exciting
is the poem.

Strictly speaking,
subtext cannot be diminished
if, as I suggest, it's infinite.
But its effect is weakened
if the reader's not encouraged
or allowed to focus on
it.

Readers cannot hope to find
the subtext if they're being hurried
on—bombarded with a constant
stream of words that are designed
to paint the picture that was more
intriguing as a sketch. That's what
I did with that haiku: I got
my explanation in before
you had a chance to find your own.

I will not say all poems must
be very short like mine. It's just
that you can kill the subtext stone
dead if you underestimate
your readers' thinking skills and drown
them in a sea of words.

know
when
to stop

You need
to cause the millstone to rotate
and bid it bear its full weight down
upon the grist: just make your readers
think.

Insofar as that's all
they do, haikus are a most effective
form.

There's one thing I've neglected
to address, though: it's enthralling

readers, capturing them, making
them obey your call to the
imagination.

Brevity,
as we have seen, is good, but breaking
off a train of thought too soon
is risky. Readers may not realise
what they are meant to do.
Before they've had a chance to tune
in to your thoughtful poetry,
it's passed them by and something new
has won them over.

You can mitigate
this risk by sacrificing
brevity.

set the wheels
in motion

You can entice
your readers to engage by hitting
them with an attention-getting
image, and not letting go
of them until you are in no
doubt that your poetry has set
the wheels of their imagination
turning with enough momentum
to sustain the thought process
beyond its kick-start motivation.

161

The aim is to broaden the extent
of the mind's eye's canvas without lessening
the scope for subtext. I'll
pursue that theme in my next chapter.

First, though, let me wrap
up the loose ends of my erstwhile
discussion: *How long should a poem
be?*

The answer's easy now:

- enough to generate a powerful
  subtext and

- make sure that the process
  of imaginative thought is under way

and no more, for the work is done.

things to do

Reflect on the *I. Why?* poem on page 154. Does it work in terms of the teaching in this chapter? Why (not)?

Write some very short poems of your own, concentrating mainly on the scope for subtext. The haiku form (p. 253) is particularly apt for this exercise: three lines of five, seven and five syllables respectively.

5c. patterns

Now we've seen how poetry connects
with the imagination through
subtext, let us consider the effects
of adding patterns.

Think of music
first: the universal language.

Universal?
Why?

Because it works
at the primeval level, circumventing
verbal reasoning and tuning
in to deeply rooted memories—
emotions, heartbeats, pitches, rhythmic
patterns—echoing
them back to us in stylised form, to tease
us, please us, set us dancing with
abandon, or to mingle
with our prevalent emotions, heightening
their intensity, manipulating

them (and us) and whipping
them into a frenzy of delight.

Poetic writing for the intellect
alone does not do these things. It
connects with feelings only indirectly,
for example if it hits
a raw nerve, so to speak, by triggering
a memory with strong emotive
links.

But when it comes to accessing
emotions, music's a more potent
force by far. So what can music tell
us about poetry?

primordial
poetry

Since all the elements
of music are reflected
in the spoken word, there can be no
doubt that there is at least some poetry
with music in it: with direct
links not just into the imagination
but to the mysterious underworld
of the emotions, through such fundamental
forces as pulsation,
volume, timbre, pitch, and the
infinity of patterns they create
in their respective variations.

164

Music is pure mathematics. We
are free to seek to elevate
the meaning to a reasoned explanation,
but this is subtext, and so
we can't be sure that anyone will share
our sense of what it means.

As poets,
all we need to do is be aware
that this mood music helps us to
enrich the subtext at a deeper level.

**patterns
enhance
subtext**

It doesn't matter that we do
not understand it: after all, we never
properly appreciate the way
that others' minds react
to anything we write or say.

We should not hesitate to use attractive
patterns in the hope
that they will help extend the scope
for subtext.

I do not mean to imply
that we cannot hope to predict
to some extent the subtext called out by
the use of patterns—music tricks
us, after all, into the emotions
that composers want to make us feel.

But the emotional appeal
of music is partly based on the association
of ideas through the intellect,
in much the same way as our minds interpret
text: a song becomes connected
with our memories of certain
times and places, and the way we felt
when we first heard it.

symbolic meaning in music

I have dealt
with such processes in sufficient detail
in my *Stirring Words* book, so
I'll say no more about them here.

The poetry
in music is what interests me
at present. Patterns are the glue
that binds it, and as poets we have much
to learn from our musician colleagues who,
through their expressive patterns, touch
our depths of feeling.

They use simple tools—

- pitch,
- rhythm,
- timbre and
- dynamic level—

166

and exploit some basic rules
to do the patterning:

- Whenever
  we hear rising pitch or bright
  sounds or a racing beat, we feel excitement,
  uplift

- and, conversely, when
  the pitch falls or the beats get slower
  or the sound grows dark, we feel a lowering
  of spirits.

Music has a sensuous
quality:

- concordant, well-tuned sounds,
  with all their ordered symmetries,
  strike us as beautifully pleasing
  to the ear,

- while we may feel profound
  discomfort or distress when we hear jarring,
  ugly noises.

The effect
of one short burst is fleeting
but it is made far
more resonant when it's projected
into the mind's ear persistently.

167

I once had the good luck to be
included in a drumming session with
about two hundred other people. We
each had a drum. We beat out rhythmic
patterns with our palms—no sticks.

The sound
of all those synchronised drumbeats was quite
impressive, but the most exciting
thing for me was the profound
effect on my emotions, which astonished
me.

I felt I that I was part
of some great, ancient monster.
Our drums were its heartbeat.
We were as one with the primordial
music of our ancient ancestors.

the mŭsĭc
ŏf spēech

Spoken language has that atavistic
power. Sounds are the subatomic
particles of speech. The rub
of clicking tongue on teeth, the hissing
sibilant, the glottal *guh*, the rounded
vowel *oo* and all the many other
sounds we make, have passed from mothers
to their countless children down
the ages since the dawn of humankind.

Speech is the resounding echo
of primeval music, redesigned
to meet the needs of each respective
age and culture.

thĕ prīmĭtīve
ĭn ūs

Speech sound is a living
image of the primitive
in us. It's in and of our bodies and
emotions.

There is music in its rise
and fall, a music that defies
our thoughtful, reasoned understanding
of the world.

As poets we must be
content to strike its chords and hope
that their effect will be to open
doors into our listeners' primeval
selves and make their spirits dance in time
with ours.

We need to see the beauty
in such things as assonance and rhyme,
despite their evident inscrutability
from our new world perspective.

We must shape our intellectual
conceits to ancient patterns. There

169

is joy in their pursuit. It's satisfying
to create a perfect
blend of thoughtful words and mathematical
expression: poetry that binds
together into one the present
world of thought with deeper resonances
from the dawn of humankind.

The poem coming next, *Arabian Days*,
is my attempt to illustrate
these points.

**poetic
proseverse**

It's just a simple
metaphor, but notice how the phraseology
is calculated
to support the imagery
with stylised speech sound.

There's the gentle
lilt of proseverse and the frequent
rhymes, but there are supplementary
patterns too, that shine out when I speak
the poem aloud.

The words are chosen
not just for their meaning but their shape—
not for the way they look on paper
but the way they work the mouth and nose.

170

- We have to work hard to produce
  the clash of patterned, consonantal assonances
  such as *glass-green*, *grass-
  green*, *brume breathed* and so on.

- The patterned use
  of *s* sounds is no less deliberate:
  such sequences of whispering sibilants
  suggest the sea.

- There's onomatopoeia
  too: the speech sounds reminiscent
  of the sounds they represent—*popped*, *whispering*,
  sinuous sufflation—

- and words that
  aren't strictly onomatopoeic,
  yet have sensory connections:
  think of *perfume*, and the way
  the lingering *oom* sound is collected
  in the nose and mouth.

See what I've done.
My metaphor says air and sea are one
with humankind and the imagination,
and I've increased its powers of evocation
beyond thought, into the primeval reach
of instincts, through the poetry of speech.

171

arabian days

I saw upon the eye-blue,
sky-blue
sea, afloat,
a grass-green,
glass-green
bottle with a note
that beckoned to my idle curiosity
to rescue it and read its message: Open Me.

In its translucent, flawless
emptiness I saw,
entrapped,
the captured
image of the sun, transcendent,
sea-drop sequined and resplendent
as if newly risen
in its glass-green prison.

Obediently I popped
the wax seal that had stopped
the captive star, whereon the brume
breathed its pelagian perfume
into my inner ear, a whispering wave
of sinuous sufflation:

You that gave
my spirit air to breathe shall be
rewarded.

You shall have the freedom
of a universe, a key
to open every door, and power of flight
beyond infinity as fast as light.

All these gifts you shall find
within the glass-green garden of your mind.

173

things to do

Study the music of language by reading aloud (or listening to) a favourite poem. Observe the extent to which the elements of music are present in the speech sound:

- pitch,
- rhythm,
- timbre and
- dynamic level.

See how many different patterns you can find running through the poem: metre, rhyme, assonance, etc.

Look also for words that have been deliberately chosen to enhance the physical experience of the speech sound, including onomatopoeic words and quasi-onomatopoeic words (such as *perfume*).

Write some poetry of your own, bringing together as many as possible of the techniques explored in these books.

book 6:

persuasive proseverse

book 6:

persuasive proseverse

If we wish to persuade our fellow
travellers to change the course
of their lives, we must use compelling
logic. We must be resourceful
too, for people do not usually
want to change.

The barriers
to changed behaviour are
deep-rooted.

What, then, can we do
to understand and overthrow
them?

See *my* answers here below.

6a. facts in action

Persuasion lies beyond the scope
of poetry, insofar
as few poets hope
to change the world.

Most often, poetry
is merely
thought-provoking.
Poets don't give clear
directions; they excite
emotions and bid memories appear
to us, but that's all.

Persuasive writers
must go further.
They invite
their audience to concur
with their analysis,
say what needs to be done and spur
their faithful listeners
on to action.

For example, politicians,
wanting to attract
sufficient votes to win a mandate,
use a battery of tactics:

- they must pander
  to the views of their electorate,

- they must prove they can handle
  current issues, showing greater
  acumen than every
  other candidate,

- and take care never
  to come across as weak
  or indecisive.

**dĕtērmĭned
effŏrt**

Such endeavours
and the wide range of techniques
employed are all directed
at the single-minded goal of seeking
votes enough to gain election.

People are not easily
persuaded. The desired effect
of candidates' persuasive reasoning
could not be simpler, yet
the expertise
required to get
the votes is far from trivial.

181

As ever, when the net
result is simple, relative
to the well formed constructive
reasoning, it's based on unequivocally
deductive
arguments.

dĕdūctĭve
rēasŏnīng

(By contrast, poetry's
inductive: outcomes must be plucked
out of the subtext, since the reasoning
is much more open-ended.)

Persuasive writers seize
upon selected facts and bend
them gently into
the intended
shape, to underpin
the chosen line of argument.

For instance (facts first):

- all the winners
  at a sports event
  come from the same locality;

facts

- it's meant
  to be an international
  event.

182

From these facts, I deduce
that:

- there is maladministration
  or, perhaps, abuse
  of power.

Without the benefit
of any more elucidation
of the facts, I might see fit
to argue that:

call to action

- the organisers
  should be forced to quit
  their posts.

This brief text over-simplifies
the situation—we'll come back
to that—but it comprises
three essential elements:

- the facts,

- conclusion(s) based on facts and, finally,

- a call to action.

Facts are the most secure point of a line
of reasoning. They should be beyond question,
truthful, anodyne
in terms of how they are expressed,

and non-judgmental, so that those who wish
to challenge or contest
our logic can't take issue
with the facts that underpin
it.

Next we set out our position.
My conclusions state where I stand in
relation to
the facts (the maladministration,
the abuse of power).

cŏnclūsĭons
jūdge
thĕ facts

Conclusions
are opinions. They reveal
not just the logic of our views
but something of our feelings
too.

My choice of the emotive
phrase *abuse of power* is an appeal
to all right-thinking people to take note
that these administrators
are, without doubt, totally
corrupt.

jūdgmĕnts
ărōuse
ĕmotĭons

What I hope is that, later
on, when I pass sentence
on them, you won't hesitate
to back whatever punishment

184

I urge and play your part in trying
to prevent
corruption.

Now that I
have got you on my side,
I specify
how these backsliders
must be punished.

These
same features may be identified
in any instance of persuasive reasoning:
conclusions from facts, leading
on to action.

That's the easy
bit. No one is likely to accede
to my suggestion
as things stand. My readers
need more facts to test
the quality
of the conclusions I've expressed
so unequivocally.

My allegations
won't stand up to scrutiny:
I speak of maladministration,
but there is no evidence

185

for the insinuation
that anything remotely reprehensible
has happened.

If it were a fact
that there had been extensive
fixing of results or blackmail,
I'd be justified
in my attack;
you would have cause to trust
my judgment and share my
disgust
at such goings-on and join the cry
for heads to roll.

My credibility
hangs on my prior
knowledge of the facts but, having said
that, facts alone do not persuade.
The facts must be interpreted,
judged and conveyed
to readers unambiguously.

conflicting
subtext

This task is made
more challenging by the enigma
of inductive reasoning.
As we have seen, new information triggers
subtext. Readers bring
their own inductive memories,

186

instinctively interpreting
the facts in their own ways, assembling
their own pictures,
thinking thoughts that are unique to them.

Since their subtext is unpredictable,
there's every possibility
that their views may conflict
with mine.

**alternative
solutions**

The same is equally
true as I try to win
support for the
enforced dismissal of the maladministrators.

Even if my readers
are of my opinion
that there's been abuse of power, they needn't
necessarily agree with my
solution.

Subtext leads
them on inductively and, try
as I may to present
my case and justify
the punishment
I'm advocating,
others may hold to dissenting
views.

187

Political debate
thrives on this constant tug of war
between the counterweighted
processes of ordered
thought: inductive and deductive
reasoning. Persuasion is notoriously
tough because we each construct
our own, unique subtext.

You'll need
an element of luck
if you are to succeed
in being persuasive. Fundamentally,
however, leading
others' thoughts takes skill, as we shall see.

things to do

Practise moving from facts to conclusions and on to
actions by adapting the example shown in this
chapter: invent new "facts", draw conclusions from
them and list the actions to be proposed in response to
your judgments. Also consider how things work in
reverse. For example, make a judgment that is
unsupported by the existing facts and consider the
additional research that would be required to support
or to undermine that conclusion.

6b. mōtǐvātǐon

Decision making's only partly
based on logic. As persuaders,
we must think in terms of winning hearts
as well as minds. Our readers must be made
to feel, as well as think, they're backing
the right choice.

Imagine buying
clothing from a shop assistant. Factually
speaking, it's so simple. Try
it on—it fits. The price is fair,
within your budget. It's just what
you need but, even as you are preparing
to pay up, you pause. There's something not
quite right.

Is it the shop assistant?
or the shop, maybe? You're just
not sure.

Instinctively you close your fist
around your money and walk out.

You trust
your logical evaluation
of the merits of the deal,
but logic does not govern motivation.
Reason merely voices an appeal
to the illiterate nerve centre
where all actions are controlled,
but reason's plan will not be implemented
if the primeval self does not uphold
the call to action.

emotions override reason

That's to say
emotions overrule persuasive
logic. Listeners will not obey
our call unless it takes account of basic
human nature.

We derive
our motivation from the prehistoric
driving forces of

- survival,

- self-improvement and

- security.

primeval motivating factors

We instinctively evaluate
all reasoned calls to action
in terms of how they might affect the balance

190

of our lives. We cannot be exactly
sure, of course, so we assess
our memories of parallel
experiences and only acquiesce
to the proposal if our instincts tell
us it presents no serious threat
to our self-interests.

The organisers
of that distant sports event are getting
their come-uppance. We can all be wise
about their fate because we're unaffected
by it.

If, by contrast,
we were falsely charged with having done
some great wrong, we'd feel anger or despondency
at least, and our instinctive   ĕmŏtīonăl
urge would be to fight to clear
our name: such feelings call on us to think   cālls
and act defensively.
                                             tŏ āctīon

Shame, anger, fear
and all such strongly negative
emotions are a powerful force
for change: we feel dissatisfied; we're driven
to attempt to redirect the course
of our emotions for the better.

191

Positive emotions, meanwhile,
militate against change: no use letting
needless, risky actions contravene
our sense of satisfaction.

Happy
and contented people do
not willingly consent to change the map
of their nice lives unless they think a new
and even brighter future beckons
onwards.

If we're to convince
them that they ought to change, we need to check
their satisfaction, challenging their instincts,
raising doubts, outlining interesting
alternatives that trigger
action.

Much advertising works by hinting
at a better life, a nicer figure,
more fulfilment, or whatever —
if you buy the product!

action
from
dissatisfaction

Such
advertisements are based upon a clever
subtext, drawn from images that touch
emotions more than intellect.
The product may be much the same

as any rival's, but if it connects
with the primeval self in a more amiable
way than others', then
that advert does the trick.

It's relatively
easy to change people's spending
patterns, but much harder to compel
them to rethink their tried and trusted
ways of living.

Take car usage,
for example. Cars are more than just
a means of transportation. They induce
extremely strong emotional
attachments:

* independence,

* privacy,

* self image...

From a logical
perspective, we see many negative
effects of urban motoring:

* congestion,

* use of fossil fuels,

* air pollution...

193

All the damaging
effects are clear: the loss of non-renewable
resources, the frustration
of the daily traffic jam,
and so on.

Our collective motivation
is apparent too.

We vote for tramways,
cycle paths, all sorts of schemes
to mitigate these problems for
the greater good of all. But we're extremely
loath to switch to public transport or,
in many cases, to change our
behaviour in the least.

Forget
the politics: this is about the power
of the emotions.

Action plans that threaten
our primeval motivations
don't proceed until the price
we'd pay is warranted by aspirations
that we choose to hold: self-sacrificing
altruism or some such
ideal shaped by the intellect.

If your persuasive writing is to touch
hard-hearted instinct, it must first connect
the hearts of readers with their minds,
and speak to both at once with symbols,
sounds and sense painstakingly aligned
in perfect harmony.

If the subliminal
mood music dances to
the urgent beat of reason's call
to action, you'll have battled your way through
the last frontier: your readers will be all
attention, ready to obey.
If you're trustworthy, you will have your way.

things to do

Consider some current controversies in the light of
this chapter. Choose stories concerned with the aim
of changing public behaviours and attitudes, paying
particular attention to the emotional obstacles that
stand in the way of change.

Put yourself in the place of an advocate for change
with respect to any of your chosen news stories, and
construct an argument that is both logically sound
and emotionally persuasive.

6c. rhetoric

Persuasive public speaking's finest hour
adorned the golden age of radio,
when suddenly the power
of oratory soared up and away
from closed debating chambers into
public consciousness.

The well-tuned disciplines
of rhetoric and the expression
of emotion through the medium
of speech are equally
well suited to the needs
of radio: great public speakers
with persuasive skills
could stir the hearts
and minds of millions—
with one voice.

The art
of rhetoric is pure persuasion. Rhetoricians
are persuasion's poets.
Their call to action is aesthetically

pleasing to the ear. They know
that listeners' emotions hold
the keys to motivation.
Therefore their unfolding
logic and their invocation
of primeval will are bound
together into one.

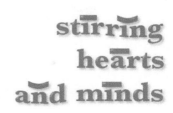

The use of patterned sound
and patterned logic are the fundamentals
of both rhetoric and proseverse:
we've learned some techniques already.
The art of rhetoric imposes
new constraints concerned with what's being said
and how the logic may be made to lead
the emotional agenda.

Let's
consider a familiar pleading:

Take more exercise and have a better
life.

The problem here is that the facts
concerning lack of exercise
are unattractive.

We must not cause apoplexy
in our listeners by dragging them
through sordid details of obesity
and ill health.

We need empathy
if they are to accept our thesis.
We can't afford the negative
emotions that are stirred
up by such unforgiving
language.

empathy

rhetorical devices
1. managing emotions

The persuader's words
and phrases are designed to raise
the spirits ever higher.

Consider one such phrase
used by reporters:

friendly fire.

This is a propagandists' trick.
It works by substituting
calming rhetoric

198

for words that might evoke the brutal
truth of warfare.

Military action
may be justified in principle,
but the inherent facts
of warfare are off-putting: people wince
at the mere thought of blood.

The politicians
and their hawkish
military colleagues
know that such emotive talk
encourages dissenting views.
They keep things positive,
if possible, by choosing
calming words that give
a coded statement of the facts.

We hear them telling us
there has been a fatal accident,
but our autonomous,
naive emotions can't help feeling
that this friendly fire
is something quite appealing,
homely, loving, warm, desirable.

This simple instance illustrates
the essence of the art of rhetoric,

Rhetorical devices for managing emotions*...

expressing an affirmative by denying the opposite

lĭtōtĕs

How can one with no delight
in language ever hope to write?

*use of words to communicate the opposite
of their usual meaning*

īrŏny

The unstressed syllable's inestimable
value can't be overstressed.

substituting one part of speech for another

āntĭhĭmēră

Memories flock
to writer's unblock.

---

* *Other rhetorical devices may also be used for this purpose.*
The categories suggested here and below are not mutually exclusive.

which is to elevate
the spirit while the intellect is set
upon a closely argued and persuasive
path.

The use of *friendly* in
this context is an antiphrasis:
that's to say that it gives up its quintessential
meaning for an opposite:
this *friendly fire* is far from friendly.

2. positive subtext

Rhetoricians' use of witty
language, likewise, is designed to send
a little blast of pleasure to
the emotions when an awkward
truth is spoken through
the coded words.

Persuasive talk
draws on a number of rhetorical
devices that
take words beyond their ordinary,
basic meanings:

- Satire,
  metaphor and irony,
  for instance, all depend

201

Rhetorical devices for positive subtext...

an extravagant statement to heighten effect

hyperbole

Master the methods of proseverse.
Hey presto! You're a different person.

self-contradicting statement

paradox

The realm of the creative mind
is broader far than humankind.

putting an inappropriate but similar-sounding word in place of the right word

malapropism

There's little point in arguing
with my destructive reasoning.

omission of one or more words

ellipsis

Beyond infinity,
the language of ideas.

on our propensity
for using subtext to extend
words into the ethereal realm of the
imagination.

- Thoughtful people
are touched by a little frisson
of delight as they unfathom deeper
meaning or decode a joke.

3. emphasis

A speech may have more impact
if the words are spoken
out of sequence.

The subliminal
effect of putting strong
or otherwise important
words first is to prolong
short term persistence: they live shorter
in the mind's eye if they're spoken later
in the sentence and then quickly
brushed off by new words with greater
impact, or by a new idea.

This trick
works in reverse as well.

Rhetorical devices for emphasising points...

reiterating a point using different words

commŏrātiŏ

Repeat your theme to strengthen its impression.
Rephrase it three or four times in succession.
Say it again: this helps to keep it fresh in
the mind's eye.

moving the last word to be the first

hystĕrŏn prōtĕrŏn

Reasoning, inductive and
deductive, leads to understanding.

building up ideas towards a pay-off

clīmăx

The tree of fruitful thought is rooted in
self-will, self-knowledge and self-discipline.

reversing the usual order of the words

hўpērbătŏn

Self-doubt
cast out.

204

If you delay
a chosen key word till the end
and build your text up to the pay-off,
you encourage listeners to extend
their subtext. The build-up helps to emphasise
your point, enhancing
its appeal to memory.

4. controlled repetition

Proseverse, with its dancing,
rhythmic repetitions and seductive
sound-plays, bears the mark of rhetoric.

Whilst the unbending structural
constraints of proseverse are too fettersome
for many writers, they,
like the above devices,
have their part to play
in the persuader's art.

Precisely
calculated plays
on sound are grist
to the persuasive
phrases radio listeners
know as sound-bites.

Rhetorical Devices for impact and memorability...

pattern of words consisting of two halves,
equally balanced but with the parts reversed in the second half

chiasmus

Be brief and apposite:
pit pithy with thy wit.

succeeding phrases of similar structure and length

isocolon

The highest heights of creativity
spring from the deepest depths of memory.

words with the same root repeated with different endings

polyptoton

A catastrophic plot 'twould be
that plotted not catastrophe.

three members linked by assonance or other similarity

tricolon

Pity the self-sensing solipsist:
unseen, unheard, unloved soliloquist.

206

Rhetoric,
like proseverse, uses patterns
to effect a quickening
of the heart that serves to gratify
the senses and support the call
to arms. Its patterns are potentially
more complex, as my small
selection clearly shows, but the essential
point remains:

persuaders can't depend
exclusively on intellectual
arguments; they must extend
the reach of their emotional effect.

things to do

Research the subject of rhetoric further. As you
review the many rhetorical devices not listed here, try
to place them within one or more of the four
categories illustrated here. Do you need any further
categories?

Create your own examples of rhetorical usage,
perhaps using one of the themes suggested here or,
better still, in support of your favourite cause.

book 7:
choosing and using
amusing ideas

book 7:
choosing and using amusing ideas

To me, at least, there's nothing half
as nice as making someone laugh.

Laughter is such a force for good.
Its power to transform the mood
of a whole room from abject misery
to joy in seconds is
a thing of wonder.

You don't need
to be a great stand-up comedian
to make 'em laugh. Just try
the simple rules below, apply
them in your writing, and you'll be
the latest thing in comedy!

7a. sŭrprīse

Think of emotional states as a spectrum.

The topmost extreme is hysteria.

Down
at the far end, depression.

Then try to connect
the two:

- laughter,

- smiles,

- well-being,

- displeasure,

- frowns,

- bitter tears.

Now imagine that there is a slider
directing one's movements within this continuum.

What are the influences that decide
the direction and speed of the slider?

We're influenced
by the events in our lives, by the people
around us, by sounds, sights, smells—everything gleaned
through the senses—
and, not least, by memories sweeping
across the mind's eye, adding context and meaning.

We think of these things as uplifting, depressing
or neither, and so our emotional state
becomes changed.

In this chapter, we'll look at the question
of structuring text to make readers elated,
or else lift up their spirits at least.

I've already
suggested that uplift is caused by

- strong beat,

- rising pitch and

- bright sounds.

There's no more to be said
about these factors, though they are well worth repeating
here. We'll stick with patterns now.

Let us consider
how babies show pleasure before they can speak.
Imagine a mother and child playing peek-a-boo.

- *Baby must wait until mother, who's hidden from view for a moment, returns. When her face reappears, baby's happy to see her.*

I dare
say that there's a profound psychological basis for baby's behaviour, but what I'm primarily interested in is the infant's reaction to subsequent turns of the game.

- *When the baby*   **expectation**
  has learnt to accept that mum always comes back and to anticipate her return, mother may become slightly more daring, by playing on that sense of anticipation and breaking the pattern: delaying a few seconds longer, emerging from some unexpected new angle, and so on.

There's no surer way to engender a surge in a baby's emotions. With little or no grasp of language, the baby still gets the joke. And this so simple example helps us understand what the essence of humour is: anticipation built up, then surprised in an uplifting way.

The repetitive pattern creates expectation. When that pattern's broken amusingly, playfully, we tend to smile, even laugh.

214

There's much more
to the subject of humour than that, but before
we examine the content, the structure and language
of humorous writing, I'd like us to stay
with the concept of patterns, for there's one more angle
we need to explore here, concerning the layering
of several patterns.

pãtterns

This text, like all proseverse,
adheres to strict patterns of rhythm and rhyme,
but there are other patterns too, subtler than those.
Unlike this metre, they don't keep strict time,
so they may be less obvious. Nevertheless
they are patterns: repetitive sounds and so on.

There are patterns of logic too. I like to press
my points home, for example, by fleshing out concepts
with visual metaphors. And there's the pattern
of self-contained chapters, with their "things to do".

I contend that such patterns, both strict and erratic,
are crucial because they enable us to
feel at ease with the text: *baby feels more secure
knowing mummy will always come back, and is free
to enjoy the game.*

You've read this far. That means you're
well tuned in to my patterns of thought and ideas.
By now you know fairly well what to expect

from my text. Whilst I hope that you're still finding new,
helpful insights, I'd like to believe you're connecting
a logical pattern of concepts that you
can use later. If I'm right, you're under the spell
of my multi-layered patterns—caught up in their tentacles.

Multiple layers assist story-telling
too. If the main story is well ornamented
with little diversions and sub-plots, it's made
so much richer, more interesting and realistic.

Each layer raises questions. The listener's persuaded
to pay close attention as long as the mystery
goes unresolved and, with so many layers
of unresolved patterns of thinking in play,
the spectrum of possible outcomes is so
much the wider.

lāyĕrĭng

*Not only does baby not know
when mum's face will appear; there is also the matter
of where she'll appear from.*

Additional patterns
increase expectation: which one will be broken
and when and how? *Even before mum comes back,
baby's laughing: the waiting is part of the joke,*
while the multiple patterns enable the cracking
of lots of small jokes, fast, one after another.
Each little joke builds the effect.

216

And then mother
delivers the punch-line: *instead of repeating*
the pattern of patterns that baby has come
to expect and enjoy, she does something completely
surprising. For instance, if this was a dumb-show
till now, mother breaks with her pattern of silence
and makes silly noises, and baby's warm smiles
turn to laughter.

Remember the peek-a-boo game.
The structure of comedy's always the same.

And here is a still more concise explanation:

- the making and breaking of false expectation.

things to do

Re-read some of your favourite comedy writing,
taking note of the things that make you smile or
laugh. Then review the text from the technical
perspective of this chapter. Identify as many different
patterns as you can, and consider the extent to which
the humour derives from the inflation and puncturing
of false expectations.

Remember that some of the patterns may be in the
subtext: the best jokes are often left to the readers'
imagination.

7b. hūmăn nātŭre

Human behaviour's by far
the most crucial ingredient of jokes.

Humour's principally based upon character.
Every comedian pokes
fun at the human condition: the way
we behave; how we look; what we say.

This obsession is hardly surprising.
It merely reflects our unquenchable
interest in people. We size
them up constantly. We express trenchant
opinions of them. We spend much
of our time interacting with them
or considering issues that touch
our relationships with them. We emulate
those whom we like or respect.
Everything that we think is connected
with human behaviour.

We form
our opinions of others according

to what we consider as normal,
and anything out of the ordinary
grabs our attention.

Normality
is, of course, wholly subjective.
It's governed by our personality
and our specific perspective
on life.

Our behaviour is founded
on patterns. We're fairly predictable,
up to a point. We are bounded
in most things we do by a strict
set of rules, often idiosyncratic
in nature and so deeply rooted
in our personality that
we don't notice them.

**patterns
of behaviour**

Yet we're acutely
aware of how others' behavioural
patterns compare with our own.
We take notice—for instance if they've
done some wrong that we could not condone,
or dressed up in an outfit we think
to be tasteless.

It's such incongruities
that make for humour: succinctly:

219

- the breaking of patterns of human behaviour in uplifting ways.

Of course, there are so many patterns
that we couldn't hope to appraise
them all here, so let's set up some categories
and start there.

I'm suggesting
that humorists use a mere handful
of simple but well tried and tested
devices. If we understand
them, we'll be so much better equipped
to write jokes or (mix in Aristotle's
POETICS) full comedy scripts.

exaggeration

Some jokes work by shining a spotlight
on one trait of character, giving
it undue importance, then mocking
it.

If a character had a proclivity
for keeping bank notes in a sock,
a plot might be contrived to suggest
that this person was wholly obsessed
with his miserly secret.

220

This focus
on one trait inevitably
makes the character unreal.

The joke
is the stronger for this. We feel free
to laugh *at* him because he's a caricature,
not a person with feelings
that might be hurt. And, insofar
as his action's repetitive, we'll
be aware of a pattern that might
be amusingly broken: say, when
the sock vanishes and we're invited
to see how he copes with being penniless.

transference

Imagine a character playing
the part of another.

Think of
a ventriloquist working a glove-puppet.
We know the puppeteer's saying
the words, but the voice that we hear
is the character's, being poured into
the puppet. The puppet appears
to be human, for all that it's thinly
disguised.

Human traits are transferred
to the puppet, and yet it remains
just a puppet.

We know it's absurd:
the absurdity partly explains
why we laugh, for this puppet becomes
a chimera, a fiction: half person,
half puppet; loquacious, yet dumb;
animated, yet lifeless.

Conversely,
for all the absurdity, we
recognise its humanity. Seeing
the character closeted in
an ill-fitting, incongruous skin,
we accept that, for all its resemblance
to somebody real, this chimera
is not to be taken too seriously.
So, however much empathy
we may feel, we are permitted
to laugh.

the chimera effect

The glove puppet's a pretty
good start, but it's not just inanimate
objects that may be used. Transference
works with two people—a man
doing girly talk, maybe—or animals
acting like humans.

222

Our miser,
for instance, might take on the guise
of a self-centred squirrel, obsessed
with the task of amassing the best
hoard of nuts in all squirreldom.

• false expectation

Few
things are funnier than someone being stupid
without realising it.

We
have the pleasure of feeling superior,
knowing this person can't see
what seems perfectly simple and clear
to us.

We enjoy trying to guess
what the outcome will be. We're delighted
when our guess turns out to be right
or if we feel the story's progressing
the right way.

There's nothing we love
more than seeing a self-centred fool
fall to richly deserved ridicule:
imagine our miser discovering
that his precious bank notes were fakes.

223

The wrong-headed include those who cheat, lie, steal, bully and so on, mistakenly thinking their wrongs go completely unnoticed.

villainy

We can't help but smile
as their dastardly plans go awry.

We're delighted to see their erstwhile
victims rise up against them in triumph.

eccentricity

But what about well-meaning, right-thinking people? They too can be funny.

Most people are flawed, at least slightly.
Humanity boasts an abundance
of quirky behaviours that make
people have a good laugh.

Eccentricity
fits this theme nicely. By breaking
with patterns of what is implicitly
held to be normal behaviour,
the harmless eccentric stands out
from the crowd. Meanwhile his or her slavish
adherence to actions that flout
the conventional wisdom attracts

the amusement of others who stick
with the norm.

• internal conflict

When a character acts
unexpectedly, our erstwhile picture
of him, her, or it may be shattered.

Imagine our miser again.

If we had grown used to his pattern
of selfish behaviour, and then
seen it suddenly changed for the better,
we'd probably feel some degree
of emotional uplift.

To get
a laugh, though, we must make sure that we
set a credible context: we must
build behavioural patterns to justify
what's going to happen.

*With only
his money to talk to, our lonely
old miser is glad when a mouse
comes to live in his dark, gloomy house.*

*His new friend, mouse, is quiet, clean, easy
to feed, and cheap: mouse likes stale cheese.*

But the miser is in for a shock
when, one evening, he pulls out the sock
from its hiding place under the bed
and finds that his mouse guest has fed
itself freely on bank notes, reducing
the miser's life savings to useless,
saliva-soaked papier maché.

I quite like that. I'm pleased with the way
that the miser has no one to blame
but himself—but life can't be the same
again.

kinetic
force

Note above all how I'm driving
the process of change by contriving
a more or less credible internal
conflict between love of money
and the pleasure of friendship.

Unfunny
as that may appear, it's intrinsically
sound, with good comic potential.
Instead of the mono-dimensional
miser, we now have a more
rounded character, well worth exploring.
This good-natured conflict has opened
him up, greatly widening the scope
for good comedy.

credibility

226

I won't pretend
that this list is complete. I'm aware
of another device I'm intending
to talk about later, and there
may be others that I have forgotten
to mention.

But what I'm suggesting
is that almost all comedy plots
are derived from and may be expressed
in these terms. And, conversely, you can
use these simple devices to craft
comic characters, and build a plan
for a plot that will make people laugh.

things to do

Listen to a favourite comedy script or read a favourite comic story in the light of this chapter. Consider the extent to which the comedy of human behaviour (as opposed to the comedy of language, which we have yet to discuss) may be explained in terms of exaggeration, transference, etc. Add your own terms to the list as necessary.

Create some characters of your own and transform them into comic characters with the help of these devices.

227

7c. lānguage

We've already discussed the unparalleled
power of language to fly
us in seconds to faraway
places.

Now I
want to focus attention on how
we can harness that power
to comic effect.

Let's begin
with the pattern of thinking
whereby our minds link
up a sequence of memories: inductive
reasoning.

As we have seen,
many words have a wide range of meanings.
When we're being bombarded
with text, it's quite hard
to establish the meaning exactly,
and so we construct

our own subtext, enacting
our own scene inductively
in the mind's eye.

As the story
unfolds, we develop
new subtext that's richer and more
realistic. We tell,
in effect, our own singular version
of what's being said,
though our thinking is led
to a greater extent by the person
who's saying the words.

misleading subtext

Comic writers
use text that misleads,
insofar as it is at least slightly
ambiguous. Readers
accede to the meaning implied
by the writer. They're tricked
into building a picture
that takes them deliberately wide
of the mark, which the writer then shatters
by giving a new,
unforeseen meaning to
what's been said up till then, and the pattern
of inductive thinking is broken.

229

The listeners or readers,
disarmed, must concede
they've been duped, and therein lies the joke.

All this happens, of course, in the blink
of an eyelid: the pictures;
the inductive thinking;
the subtext that sets up the trick
of the word-play.

**instant
comedy**

Such speed is a dominant
feature of language-based comedy.
Contrast the slow
build-up that we must go
through with characters.

Patterns of language
are so much more fluid
than patterns of human
behaviour. Words have such a tangle
of meanings that they can transport
us in seconds, along the most tortuous
pathways, to vistas
that need not exist
in reality.

Stand-up comedians
and radio writers
exploit this fact, duping us, leading

our thoughts on at lightning
speed.

Nothing's impossible on
the ineffable retina
of the mind's eye, with its inconstant,
capricious, unfettered
imaginings.

By contrast, visual
images based on the physical
realm of things actual
tend to distract
our thoughts, slowing them down to the pace
of the real world, restricting
them to a much narrower space
and outshining the pictures
in our mind's eye.

**all in
the mind**

This matters little
in character comedy,
which is predominantly
based on real life, but it
impedes language-based humour, which is
not intrinsically visual,
since it is purely symbolic:
language comedy's all
in the mind.

231

Please don't think I'm suggesting
that language and character
comedy are
incompatible and, therefore, best
kept apart. On the contrary, they
are inseparable.

Take,
for example, that timeless mainstay
of so much mischief-making:
misunderstanding: one character's
words or deeds are
misinterpreted by
someone else.

Happily for us, scientists
haven't discovered a way
yet to work out what's going
on in our heads, so
that, unless we explicitly say
what we hope to achieve by our actions
or words, no one can
tell for sure what our plan
is.

By piecing together the facts,
they can hope to draw their own conclusions,
but it's usually guesswork,
with several answers to choose

from, and several key questions
unanswered.

ambiguity

In short, ambiguity
rules, and when two
or more people have different views
of the facts, their conclusions
may well be at odds.

This phenomenon—
misunderstanding—
is widely exploited in comedy
writing:

- *A bland,*
  saintly character and well-meant, innocent
  actions are viewed
  by another as having a sinister
  purpose.

- *A lewd*
  womaniser discovers too late
  that the beautiful, sweet-natured,
  fun-loving creature
  that he has asked out on a date
  is no woman at all, but a man.

But as often as not
in a comedy plot
there are layers of misunderstanding.

If A is mistaken as to
the intentions of B,
the confusion may well be a mutual
one.

crŏssed
pūrpŏsĕs

And if three
or more characters add their own brands
of mistaken intentions,
the pattern of misunderstanding
expands exponentially.

Such is the principal feature
of farce, with its tangle
of intrigue and deceitful
crossed purposes. This is the language
of misunderstanding
writ large. Every character's devious,
each of them bandying
words with the aim of deceiving
the others, and, maybe, the audience
too.

As objective
outsiders we're given a broader
and more circumspect
view of what's going on.

But yet farther
off, in full command,

sits the writer, who makes sure the characters'
misunderstandings
engage with the audience, eliciting
subtext that leads
audience members, in their turn, to misunderstand.

Subtext feeds
ambiguity. Comedy thrives
on this simple fact.

When
writing comedy, then, you should strive
to find words that leave plenty
of room for uncertainty.

- Play
  with your audience. Lead them astray.

- Gain their interest by building up plausible
  logical patterns that cause
  them to grasp the wrong end of the stick.

- Break their patterns of thought—

  and the trick
  is complete.

sea change

The owl and the pussycat grabbed the loot, boarded
the getaway pea-green boat, cast off and oared
it as fast as they could.

They were rich, their marauding
days done. They might soon be exposed as the fraudsters
they were, but by then they'd be living abroad
in the tropical sun.

As they hastened toward
the wide ocean and freedom, they laughed and applauded
their triumph: the biggest haul ever recorded!

Far, far out, night fell. They felt they could afford
to relax. Their professional ice-coolness thawed
in their sultry seclusion, as something primordial
stirred.

It was Pussy who started the bawdy
talk. Owl, talons velvet-gloved, playfully clawed
his friend Pussy's intemperate zone. Pussy pawed
the Owl's outcrop, and all that night long they explored
one another's... I think I should spare you the sordid
details.

236

Six days passed, and by now Owl was lording
it over her.

She was annoyed that he snored
in his sleep like a badly tuned, steam-powered accordion.

He loathed her meaningless chatter: she jawed
non-stop.

She couldn't stand the weird way that he gnawed
at his food.

He despised her obsessive, inordinate
grooming and futile retouching of gaudy
fur highlights.

She couldn't put up with his mordant,
smug, Wise-Owl critique of what he called her flawed
personality.

Bitterly rueing her tawdry
affair, Pussy stole out of bed that night, dawdled
amidships to where all the loot had been stored
and, taking in hand an antique silver sword,
lunged at Owl, full blade. He rolled over. She'd scored
a direct hit, but it was the hull that she gored,
not the Owl, who snored on as the sea water poured
in, and dragged down boat, Owl, Cat and ill-gotten hoard.

237

things to do

Study *Sea Change*. Observe how it is based not only on the comic writing techniques explored above, but also on principles established previously (plot, evocative language, etc). Identify as many techniques as you can, and consider their respective contributions to this retelling of *The Owl and the Pussycat*.

Practise the techniques for yourself, as follows:

- Create two or more characters.

- Devise conflicting motives for them, which are likely to give rise to misunderstanding.

- Think of a comic surprise to end your story.

- Devise layers of patterns that will engage the attention of your readers or listeners.

Sea Change was inspired by the image of the miser and, in particular, the rhyming possibilities for the word *hoard*. I was intrigued to find so many non-identical rhymes and began listing words that might help tell a coherent and amusing story in proseverse. Reflecting on *pawed* and *clawed*, I thought of *The Owl and the Pussycat*. Within a couple of hours, *Sea Change* had written itself.

book 8:
inspiration
by limitation

book 8:
inspiration by limitation

One of the most surprising
pleasures of the job
of writing is devising
thought-provoking problems
to be solved. They stimulate
your mind and make you more creative.

In this last book, I explore
techniques to make your writing more
inspired: how, by imposing limitations
on yourself, you fire your imagination.

păddў gŏrmlĕў

8a. cōnstrāints are ŭsefŭl

Creativity
is fundamentally
inductive: without free
association, we
could never have ideas.

The creative process
does not end there, though:
we must be circumspect,
self-critical, selective.

The glorious irony
of creativity,
to my mind, is that it
is largely analytical:
ideas spring up easily;
the deductive reasoning—
that turns the first idea
into something interesting

244

and properly thought through—
is harder work to do.
That hard work holds the key
in terms of quality
control.

dĕdūctĭve thīnkĭng gŏvērns qualĭtȳ

Creative freedom
can be like meandering
around a city,
walking streets at random.
With some luck you'll hit
upon something exciting.
Then again you might
not. You need to take care
to move towards somewhere
you think you'd like to go.
Of course you cannot know
for sure how good it will
turn out to be until
you've walked around.

Creative
writers find this too.
You can't be sure if you
have got a really great
idea till you've done
some writing—a few hundred

245

words, perhaps (unless
you're planning to express
yourself in fewer still).

The fundamental skill
at work here is the setting
of constraints. By narrowing
your scope, you are
ensuring that you get
somewhere.

constraints
fuel creativity

You set your sights
upon one path, and lights
appear by magic, guiding
you along the way.
And, as you write, deciding
what you want to say,
your sentences refine
your thinking further to
a still more narrow line
of logic.

It is through
this process—limiting
our field of exploration
and then focusing
upon one destination—
that we find our voice.

246

So it should not seem strange
that limiting our choices
in terms of the range
of writing tools at our
disposal should be no
less useful in empowering
thought.

Constraints do slow
us down, it's true: composing
verse, with all its rules,
is harder work than prose.
With high precision tools
like rhyme and metre, every
word must justify
its place.

Prose writers never
really need to try
to scrutinise each syllable
with so much care.

Verse writing is more skilful.
It is this awareness
of the many attributes
of words—sense, length,
sound, rhyme and metre—that
is the verse writer's strength.

Constraints force us to think
more deeply, search more widely
for good rhymes or linking
words that fit inside
the framework of our scheme.
That thinking is extremely
beneficial, as we'll see,
in terms of quality.

things to do

Consider the importance of constraints in your daily life. When we have the freedom to choose from many activities, we cannot begin to decide what to do until we narrow down the field of choices.

Choosing where to go for a day out is an obvious example: we start by narrowing the range of choices to places within reach that we would like to visit; then, perhaps, we narrow further to places that may not be too crowded; and so on.

Think of other examples of ways in which constraints shape our lives. Sketch the decision processes whereby we go about choosing from a vast range of options.

248

8b. pŏētĭc fōrm

Verse writers have to learn to face
the fact that even their most basic
resource—sound—is governed
by a number of
acute constraints, for verse technique
demands that syllables are sequenced
within pre-ordained
and carefully constrained
sound patterns: each stressed syllable
among so many unstressed syllables,
with frequent rhyming
words that mark the time
by acting as a sort of signpost
at the end of every line.

Poets have shaped these
rules over centuries
into specific forms that are
constrained within a still more narrow
range of options.

Normally,
poetic form
dictates three things. They are:

poetic constraints

- The metre:
  the stressed syllables (or *feet*)
  per line;

- The rhyme scheme: that
  is, the specific pattern
  of the rhyme words—which lines share
  rhyme sounds with which and how they pair
  off;

- And the length—the number
  of lines per verse, or sometimes
  in the whole piece.

Let me illustrate
the point with some established forms:

limerick

The limerick form is petite.
It begins with two lines of three feet.
These give way to a new
rhythm: two lines of two
feet. Then three feet more make it complete.

tĕrză rĭmă

The ancient Italian verse form, terza rima,
encourages use of a much wider range
of rhyme words, with the help of a chain rhyming scheme.

Chain rhyme is a means of effecting a change
in one rhyme sound while keeping another one going.
Line 2 of each stanza concludes with a strange

rhyme, while lines 1 and 3 use a rhyme that we know
from the previous stanza. This scheme is effective
in binding the stanzas together, to flow

in a seamless progression with inter-connecting
rhyme sounds all the way. You can have two or more
three-line stanzas—lots more—but you're always expected

to finish the piece with a stanza of four
lines: the first three maintain the same scheme and declare
a new rhyme, while the fourth brings an end to the story
and rounds off the scheme with a last rhyming pair.

villánelle

A gently turning carousel
with rhymes and rhythms that repeat:
this form is called the villanelle.

It's like the tolling of a bell,
so clear and steady is the beat:
a gently turning carousel.

The stanza length is good for telling
stories: three lines of four feet.
This form is called the villanelle.

The main rhyme sound—in this case *ell*—
starts each verse and makes it complete:
a gently turning carousel.

A second rhyme occurs as well,
once in each stanza—here it's *eat*.
This form is called the villanelle.

The formal use of parallel
refrains constrains length, short and sweet.
A gently turning carousel,
this form is called the villanelle.

haīkū

Haikus make a mean- — 5
ingful point in seventeen — +7
syllables in all. — +5
—
=17

(Stressed syllables may fall
in any pattern, so, unlike
the other forms shown here, the haiku
is not ruled by metre.
When we don't need feet,
we don't need rhymes.
The haiku breaks
the rules in this sense, and it makes
the point that rules are fluid.)

As a writer, you
are free to work within a known
poetic form or make your own
rules.

You may choose to stick
with all the rules, or pick
the ones that suit you—such as chain

chōose
yŏur ōwn
cōnstraīnts

rhyme, or the use of a refrain—
and use them in a new
form of your own.

Nor do
you ever need to work with these
established forms. If you can please
yourself by writing verse
in some form that is personal
to you, the chances are
that you will not be very far
from pleasing others through
the writing that you do.

things to do

Try writing within the constraints of verse forms such
as these.

Research other poetic forms. Observe the extent to
which they are governed by similar constraints to
those described here (metre, number of lines, rhyme
schemes, use of refrains, etc).

Devise your own verse forms and experiment with
them.

8c. stōrў līne

Poetic form's primarily
concerned with governing
sound patterns: when and where
the stresses fall and how to bring
the poem to a graceful
end.

However challenging
you may find the constraints of placing
syllables within a tightly
ordered framework, metrical
constraints won't help you if
your goal is better
text. To do that, you'll need different,
additional
sets of constraints concerned with sense—
and sound, but principally
sense. For what a difference
it makes when sense and sound
combine to show true eloquence
of speech.

Initial groundwork
is the key: deciding what
you want to say and how
to say it.

Story-line and plot,
and so on, act as powerful
constraints. The basic
facts of story-line
or plot are like a sort of casement
that serves to define
the general shape. This shape dictates,
to quite a large extent,
the range of words used to create
the text and the events
to be described.

plōt
acts as a
constraint

To illustrate
the point, let me devise
a simple story-line and use
it as an exercise
in writing.

First, I'll have to choose
a starting point. And luckily
I've thought of an amusing
little phrase that struck
me as a possible refrain:

256

Susanna's hair was green.

By using it, I will constrain
the structure and the meaning.
The challenge will be to maintain
the interest of my readers
throughout every repetition
of that line. I'll need
to give it structure, and position
it in such a way
as to enable the addition
of more lines that say
something to us about Susanna
and her hair.

ă rĕfraīn
thāt cŏnstraīns

I find
that writing words is easier than
adopting pre-designed
shapes. I prefer to let my plan
evolve its own shape.

I
have got some lines to try:

*Her Dad, who knew
a thing or two...*

This strikes me as quite promising.
I like the lively beat,
although it's fairly challenging
to rhyme lines of two feet.

These lines have got me wondering
what sort of explanation he
might offer for green hair. Let's see:

Susanna's hair was green.

Her Dad, who knew
a thing or two,
observed that grandpa
was a Scandinavian
with yellow-golden
hair, while old
Aunt Flo had told
Susanna's brother
her grandmother
used blue rinse
for years, and since
yellow and blue
make green, then who
was to deny
that might be why
Susanna's hair was green?

It took me quite a while
to write that, but I'm pleased with it
because it makes me smile.

I'm glad I didn't have to fit
the words into too fixed
a structure: that might be a bit
too much!

I guessed the mixed-
up colours ought to be a good
idea; then I pictured
the blue rinse and thought that would
be fun too; and I'd stick
with short lines—lines of two feet shouldn't
be *too* hard to write.

Notice how the story line
is subject to some tight
constraints already. The proclivities
of the relations
(the blue rinse and so on) give
us every indication
that we're talking comedy
here; and, now we've met Dad,
we ought to meet the family.

If that's so, I must add
at least another two or three

259

or even four new verses,
each considering the green
hair from a different person's
point of view.

Dad's thoughts have been
extremely useful, though
he hasn't really set the scene
for us. We need to know
one fact above all others: where
Susanna stands.

- *Was this
  her natural colour?*

- *Was green hair
  her choice?*

- *Or was it mischief?*

There's no doubt which I prefer:
the *mischief*. Stories thrive
on conflict.

If Susanna hates
green hair, we'll have a lively
story. Her dislike creates
a mystery to hold
the reader, who anticipates
the story to be told.

Susanna's hair was green.

It was most strange.
Why should it change
like that? She'd gone
to bed a blonde
and then this weird
green hair appeared
all suddenly.
No wonder she
was mystified.
She cried and cried:
Susanna's hair was green.

By now the plot is fairly well
defined.

I can foresee
that there will be three basic elements:

- *the mystery,*

- *the revelation that will tell*
  us how the green hair came
  about

- *and something in between.*

The very simplest framework
would dispense with intervening
text and tell us straight
away what made the hair turn green.

But this would just deflate
the story and the comedy.
We need more text, not less.
Our readers (listeners) want to be
kept waiting while they guess
the answer to the mystery.

**keep
the readers
guessing**

The "something in between"
creates that waiting time. It must
be relevant and meaningful,
though. It is more than just
a padding. It must give
fresh detail that supports the thrust
of the main narrative.

The verse about the father plainly
serves this purpose fairly
well. It steers close to the main
theme—that's to say the hair—
but it is there to entertain,
not to inform.

Even so,
it won't do on its own. I'll need
at least one more to go
with it. I want to keep my readers
waiting, guessing where
the story's going to lead.

My finished text is there
on the next page. You'll see I've added
two more verses. Mum's
been slotted "in between" with Dad,
and finally there comes
the mischief.

I think it's not bad.

things to do

Think about the precise constraints governing the "in between" verses, and try adding another verse based on the same principles.

Develop your own verse story, gradually constraining the plot in broadly the same way as this chapter describes.

263

susanna's hair

Susanna's hair was green.

It was most strange.
Why should it change
like that? She'd gone
to bed a blonde
and then this weird
green hair appeared
all suddenly.
No wonder she
was mystified.
She cried and cried:
Susanna's hair was green.

Susanna's mum
tried hard to comfort
her by telling
her how well
the green hair suited
her, how beautifully it
would match her pretty
new dress, and
how she would stand
out from the crowd
of plain-haired, dowdy
girls, and how
she'd surely wow
the whole world, now
Susanna's hair was green.

Her Dad, who knew
a thing or two,
observed that Grandpa
was a Scandinavian
with yellow-golden
hair, while old
Aunt Flo had told
Susanna's brother
her grandmother
used blue rinse
for years, and since
yellow and blue
make green, then who
was to deny
that might be why
Susanna's hair was green?

Susanna's brother
was another
matter. He
decidedly
disliked his sister—

never missed
a chance to get
her all upset.
The previous week
she'd done a sneaky
thing: she took
his football book
and plastered sticky
girly pictures
onto every
page—Not clever!
For his sweet
revenge, he treated
her shampoo
with some strange, blue
concoction taken
from her make-
up kit, and waited.
It was great,
an excellent
experiment:
Susanna's hair was green.

8d. ūnlĭmītĕd limĭtātĭon

Plot, rhyme and metre are significant
constraints, but hundreds
more exist. It's difficult
enough to list them, let
alone provide specific
instances. You'll get
a clearer picture if I choose
a few.

The alphabet's
A good one. I find using
Letters formulaically
Productive and amusing.
Here, say, you can see
A code word—ALPHABET—appear
By reading downwards. The
Effect is but the merest
Trifle when compared with that

of verse upon the ear.
The use of coded patterns
certainly constrains the writer,
but it doesn't matter
more than very slightly
to the reader.

The writing benefits,
in terms of heightened
intellect and mental
discipline, should not be overlooked,
though.

**cŏnstrāints
fŏr cārefŭl
wrītĭng**

- Every sentence
  has to undergo
  exceptionally careful scrutiny,
  far down below
  the surface.

- The minutest
  issue—where to place a single
  letter—can uproot
  a whole day's work or bring
  the project to its knees.

Even so,
I like such challenging
constraints.

I'd like to show
you what it's like to take things to
extremes (if you don't know
already): a haiku
that obeys the usual
constraints—says something true,
profound and meaningful
in only three short lines of five
and seven and five syllables.

To make it livelier,
I'll try to rhyme (Haikus
don't need to) and contrive
if possible to use
all the letters of the alphabet.

Rhyming haikus are
considered irregular—
Some might say bizarre!

My first step is to choose
some words containing letters
x, *y*, *z* and maybe *q*.
I'd probably regret
it if I left these too
late (*z* especially—it is
perhaps the rarest)... *Zoo*,
unzip, blaze, dazzle, quiz
(now there's a good one: *quiz* takes care
of *z* and *q* too), *wizard*,
zeal...

**toughest
constraints
first**

268

Three words must share
a rhyme as well. I might use *eeze*
and get the z in there
that way:

Don't expect to squeeze
every letter in with ease.
I've just managed these.

That has no b's
or f's or k's, but it's no bad
start: twenty-three's
a good score to have had
first time.

It lacks profundity,
though, which is rather sad,
since it can't properly
be called a haiku. I'm forgetting
that it's poetry
I'm writing—No use fretting
over rhyming sounds and chasing
after letters yet.

What I need is a basic
theme—something I want to say.
Once I've got that in place,

269

I can begin to play
with words.

I wonder if I ought
to make my poem convey
what a haiku is?

A thought
set down on paper—that's good.

Captured—
better still—and brought
out proudly and unwrapped
and shown to everyone.

No—this
is it: it's frozen, trapped
in ice—some sort of crystal.

Amber—wonderful: opaque,
yet lustrous and persistent.

Thoughts crystal-jewelled
Exquisite amber dewdrops
Sunlight blazing through   *(No f, k or v)*

270

Thoughts, quick, given flight.
Crystals, fixed in amber bright,
shine with dazzling light.   *(No j or p)*

Thought's primeval flight
quickly fixed in amber bright
blazing jewelled light   *(All the letters!)*

I felt quite sure I'd make
it once the amber came to mind.

But was it a mistake,
that last constraint of finding
room for every letter? Maybe.
I was less inclined
to say what I should say
than to choose words to fit my scheme
and use them anyway.

But then these were supremely
difficult constraints, to illustrate
just how extreme
you can be.

Yet I still
think that last haiku isn't quite
my style, though it fulfils
all my constraints. I think I'll write
it once more with some slight
adjustments.

Thought's primeval flight
frozen fixed in amber bright
dazzling ammonite

index

discovery (as an element of plot), 69-70
dissatisfaction as a motivating factor, 191-193
dynamic level (see *volume*)

E
eccentricity, 224-225
ellipsis, 202
emotional spectrum, 212-213
emotions
  lowering, 167
  persuasive argument, 184-185, 189-195
  poetry, 151-152, 163-171
  uplift, 167, 213, 220
  (see also *evocative language, patterns* & *rhetoric*)
empathy, 198, 222
emphasis, 203-205
enjambment
  conventional (mid-phrase), 45, 57
  proseverse (mid-word), 53
engaging the imagination, 59, 132-134, 150, 257
  (see also *subtext*)
equilibrium (as the enemy of storytelling), 60
evocative language 116-120, 128-129, 133, 152
exaggeration, 220-221
expectation (see *anticipation*)

U
unexpected behaviour, 225-226

V
villainy, 224
villanelle, 252
visceral language, 128-129
volume, 164, 166
vowel sounds, 23-24

about the author

Paddy Gormley has been writing professionally for more than forty years, with articles in publications as diverse as *Music & Musicians* and *Financial Times*.

He has extensive experience of teaching creative and analytical thinking and writing skills, including Crisis (2005-2018) and Blackheath Conservatoire (2000-2004). His interest in Aristotelian reasoning, apparent here in *Constructive Induction*, dates from the late 1980s, when he worked as a problem-solving skills trainer for a management consultancy firm.

Three of his verse plays have been professionally produced in London: his proseverse showpiece *2020 Visions* (OSO Barnes 2019), *The Social Climber* (adaptation of Molière's *Le Bourgeois gentilhomme*, Upstairs at the Gatehouse 2012), and *Hamlet, Tragedy of a Fat Man* (Etcetera Theatre & tour 2002-2003).

2020 Visions was adapted for radio and produced in 2021-2.